10·17·79

WORKING FOOD

PARENT BOOK

Adeline Garner Shell
Kay Reynolds

 Sovereign Books • New York

Also by Adeline Garner Shell and Kay Reynolds

Brown Bagging It: The Lunch Box Idea Book
Feel Better After 50 Food Book

Published by Sovereign Books
A Simon & Schuster Division of
Gulf & Western Corporation
Simon & Schuster Building
1230 Avenue of the Americas
New York, New York 10020

Designed by Irving Perkins
Manufactured in the United States of America

10 9 8 7 6 5 4 3 2 1

Library of Congress Cataloging in Publication Data

Shell, Adeline Garner.
Working parent food book.

Includes index.
1. Cookery. 2. Food. I. Reynolds, Kay,
1911-   joint author. II. Title.
TX652.S494   641.5   79-16290

ISBN 0-671-18439-3
ISBN 0-346-12421-2 pbk.

Dedicated to all you gallant people—working women and working men—who are cooking, keeping house, and bringing up children while away at work all day. May this book make it easier and more satisfying for you.

Contents

1

Working Parent Cook

"The worst thing you have to do in a working day is to get dinner at the end of it! What a hassle."

That's what working parents have told us, coast to coast.

And then they ask: "Couldn't it be easier?"

The answer is yes. We offer three options. Why three? Because we have found that working parents fall into three groups: those who like to cook, those who are indifferent to it, and those who can't stand it.

For people who like to cook and who don't mind spending a reasonable amount of time doing it, we offer the Accordion Recipe (meat for three meals in one cooking) plus Do Ahead Time to make cooking more efficient and to guarantee meals with real homemade taste and good nutrition. For people who neither like nor dislike cooking but want to do it as simply as possible, we offer Q&Es, quick and easy dishes made with good food in short order. For those who detest cooking, we offer TTMs, throw together meals, made with ready-bought, prepared foods but put together in a way that makes a nourishing meal. This will take some of the strain off people who dislike cooking, but it's not a total answer to making meals.

The best solution for the working cook is to combine all the above options as time and energy permit after a working day. Cook ahead when you can, fill in with Quick and Easy dishes, and in the last extreme of fatigue, serve a Throw Together Meal.

Recipes Designed for Working Parents

Our recipes are designed for busy people who have to get meals on the table fast after a long, hard working day. All the extra steps, fuss and fume, needless dishes, pots, and pans to wash, have been eliminated. These recipes are stripped to essentials, yet they turn out lively tasting dishes with good nutrition. No recipe-writing jargon here. The recipes are expressed in simple language to get on with the job of cooking in the fastest, easiest way. In fact, we believe these recipes are so clear, any child who can be trusted to be alone in a kitchen can cook with them as successfully as a grown-up. Lots of children in families of working parents are cooking nowadays, and we had these children in mind as well as adults.

Cooking is a cluster of little actions, of processes. Each can take less time and effort if done efficiently. Efficiency has been our concern, even to choosing cooking utensils that combine processes rather than calling for extra bowls, mixers, and measuring cups. Our recipes are purposely planned to cut dishwashing and cleanup to the minimum. You'll discover this as you cook with them. We want to liberate you from the kitchen as much as possible. Our equipment section, chapter 9, is a guide to cookware that makes it easier for the working parent to cook and serve.

Invest Cooking Time for Good Dividends

We guarantee that if you'll set aside only two hours a week, you can plan and prepare the basic foods for several days' meals. They will all be ready in the refrigerator when parents come home tired from work. On any workday night, a relaxed twenty minutes to a half-hour will serve a fine home-cooked meal to the family. We call this plan "Do Ahead Time." It's the time to do things like preparing salad greens for a week's meals. The greens will stay crisp and refreshing if stored correctly. Do Ahead Time is chopping onions and green peppers and refrigerating them, ready to season dishes with fresh flavor instead of that tired, dehydrated taste.

And it's preparing meat ahead for three meals at one time, using our Accordion Recipes. This is the best way to make your kitchen nice to come home to, and the evening meal pleasure time for all of the family, including you.

The Accordion Recipe

When we set out to make it easier for working parents to cook good meals at the end of a working day, we developed the Accordion Recipe. It stretches to make cook-ahead meat courses for three delicious meals. And we found a way to do this without any flavor fatigue on the family's part. Though the meats are cooked in advance, there is no "leftover" taste.

Here's an example. During Do Ahead Time, a pork roast is cooked. It is served plain for the first meal. What could be better? The rest of the meat is refrigerated for two quick meals on busy weeknights. But you don't have plain roast pork turning up twice again with this plan. Instead, you serve sliced pork heated in a delectable and extremely easy, zesty, homemade sauce, a complete flavor change. The sauce is so simple, it's made in the same pan in which the meat is heated. Now for the secret of eliminating that leftover taste. The meat is heated ever so gently and slowly while you prepare the vegetable and the rest of the meal. Only low heat is used in readying these cooked meats for second and third appearances at the table. We assure you the subsequent dishes will taste brand-new and fresh-cooked.

For a third meal, the pork is cut into slivers to make

a savory Chinese Pork Fried Rice dish to delight children and grown-ups alike.

Some of the Accordion Recipes are made with meats such as chopped beef and sausage that cook in less time. These can be cooked while a family is having dinner instead of in Do Ahead Time.

So there you have it: the Accordion Recipe, meat for three meals in one easy cooking time, for three delicious, homemade meat dishes that cut last-minute preparation and cooking time. This also eliminates those "What'll I serve in a hurry" worries for the homegoing working parent. It's all planned. And it's all delicious. No more makeshift meals.

You will find five of these new Accordion Recipes to make life a lot simpler and more enjoyable. Accordion Recipes are given for pork, ground beef, chicken, sausage and roast beef. It's wise to remember that when foods are stored in the refrigerator for more than three days, the temperature must be 40° F.

Q&Es

Our Quick and Easies aren't just a matter of opening cans and packages, although we do call on convenience foods when they are good-tasting, nutritionally worthwhile and reasonably priced for the convenience offered. Our Q&Es rely more on revolutionary ways to cook. Our Macaroni and Cheese dish is not made with a mix. It's homemade, but in a different way. The whole thing is done in one pot—you boil the macaroni, which sauces itself when cheese and milk are added. It's so good, so nourishing, the easiest thing in the world to cook, and only one pan to wash!

Our Ham and Sweet Potato Q&E dinner is also made in one pan, including the green bean vegetable. The cooked ham (it could be your own leftovers, bought, sliced cooked ham, or canned ham) is sliced and sautéed lightly in a large skillet and pushed to one side. Then canned sweet potatoes are added, seasoned with cinnamon and fruit juice, and heated. Finally, drained canned beans are added to heat. A meal in one skillet that is good-tasting, very nutritious, and a snap to do.

Some Q&Es take a little more cooking, but they have all been simplified to reduce effort to the vanishing point. Yet, there has been deep concern for nutrition. In many cases, menus, carefully worked out to give a balanced meal, are provided with the recipes.

TTMs

Throw Together Meals are the cook's court of last resort. They might be a cold meal, a plate of sliced roast beef, potato salad, coleslaw (from the store), tomato wedges, good bread, milk to drink for each member of the family, and fresh fruit for dessert. That's a nutritionally balanced meal. It's expensive, but it's a better meal nutritionally than a fast-food meal or some of the take-out pizzas. The Throw Together Meals are planned for nutritional balance, so use them "as is" to give your family the nutrients they need even when you are too tired to cook.

If you look over some of the Q&Es, you will find that

they are almost as easy as TTMs. When you serve them, your family will enjoy better food and more variety in their meals.

What Makes a Meal?

Because working parent families often eat outside the home—and sometimes not full meals—it's important that dinner, the main meal, be really nourishing. The chapter "What Makes a Meal?" takes the mystery out of nutrition. Follow this simple advice and the family will enjoy increased vitality, and you will very likely cut down on doctor's bills and prescriptions, too.

Haste makes waste in nutrition as well as in other ways. Our special menus take a lot of the tension out of the main meal. When the children are irritable—and driving the working parent bananas with hunger complaints—try our "holding pattern" trick. While you are making dinner, sit the folks down to the table to enjoy a nourishing, easy first course that is not just an empty snack but a planned part of the main meal. A small cup of soup and a piece of toast is a good example; or a finger salad of cucumber spears, carrot chunks and cheese strips with a piece of crunchy bread holds off hunger till the main course. It tastes good, and does good because the foods carry important nutrition. With the kind of easy main courses presented here, you, too, will in most cases be able to sit down to the table and enjoy the "holding pattern" foods, easing up your own hunger and tension. If not, take the first course to the stove and munch while you cook.

The Kitchen, Friend or Enemy

Most kitchens are not arranged to do cooking in the least possible time with the least effort. Many people spend more time getting ready to cook than they do cooking. That seems odd, but think about it and you'll find it's true.

Start watching yourself cook. Are you retracing your steps often as you reach for this and that? Are materials grouped for easy access, for getting right down to business on a cooking process? Or must you dart here and there, making a pattern like an old-fashioned maze, and wasting much precious time and energy?

Very simple changes in your kitchen—for example, a mere shift of certain foods and utensils to form work centers related to specific cooking tasks—won't require expensive renovations and can make all the difference. You'll find out all about it in chapter 2, "Your Kitchen, Friend or Enemy?"

Freezers Can Help

Many working parents make marvelous use of a freezer. Others manage quite well with only their refrigerator freezing compartment though that cannot be depended upon for long-term storage as a freezer can.

It's efficient to make a double batch of a favorite main dish such as a casserole, serve one and freeze the other. It takes know-how to get the most from a freezer in terms of quality food, nutrition return, and efficient storage. How you use the freezer is your choice.

Part-Time Cooks

Fathers whose children come to stay with them periodically need special, easy recipes or quick ways to serve food that allow them to make the most of the time they have with their children, keep the kids well fed, and the parent at a nonfrantic level.

In chapter 6, "Just for Fathers," there are suggestions for handling this special problem. For instance, when children stay over, both parent and kids can put the makings of a good breakfast in the cupboard and refrigerator the night before. Rising time is up to the individual. It makes a nice, leisurely start for the day.

Lunch will probably be eaten out, but kids get tired and look forward to coming home to a cozy, hearty dinner at night. This can be very easy with our special strategies and tips.

Your Assets, Your Children

Children can be dividends or drawbacks in the kitchen. The choice is yours.

Even very little children can be trained to set the table every day, help clear it, and scrape the plates ready for washing. This may take a little rearranging of cupboards or shelves. The needed dishes and cutlery for dinner should be placed on low shelves in a cupboard or bookcase within a child's easy reach for setting the table. He or she can also put the things away easily if they are at this level.

This kind of work may call for a suspension of "perfect" standards in order to get it done. A little child does not always put silver in the right position but the table does get set, and that's the real name of the game in a busy, working parent household.

Older children, if trustworthy and trained in kitchen safety, can put things in the oven ahead of a parent's arrival from work, scrub potatoes, prepare vegetables ready for cooking, assemble salad, and get out the pots, pans and utensils needed for cooking a particular meal.

Older children can take out the garbage, keep the kitchen clean, straighten cupboards, wipe down the stove, and do other kitchen chores. Working parents are bringing their children many extra benefits by holding a paying job. Parents need have no hesitation in asking the children to help make a home when they are contributing so much to it.

Most families find that a chart system works best, with tasks assigned on a rotating basis, and a checkoff provided for when the task is done. Many people tie chores to allowances for their children. It seems only fair that when children do chores of this magnitude in the home, they should be compensated and buy what they like with their money. This, of course, is a matter for each family to decide.

Far from feeling guilty about children doing jobs around the house, the working parent might better feel that she or he is giving the child the most priceless gift, the ability to achieve and be independent, to know how to maintain the essentials of practical living on his own. That will stand the child in good stead for a lifetime.

Young Marketers

Children can be a wonderful help during big shopping trips, which can be organized not only to save time and effort but also to save money. The most successful shopping families we know put their children in charge of special groups of food or household needs. One child shops for bread, crackers, cookies, etc.; becomes thoroughly familiar with quality and prices in this area; and can do a fine job of comparison shopping to get the best for the money. Another specializes in all detergents, laundry, and other household supplies needed; and is a whiz in checking price comparisons in this area by weight, cents off, coupons, or other arrangements, to make the best choice. Still another child checks canned goods for quality and prices, or the specialty may be in checking canned, dried and frozen varieties of the same food to determine the best buy. This kind of family "togetherness" makes the kids sharp shoppers— a necessary skill in these times of inflation—and it takes a great deal of strain off the working parent.

Other Helps to Call Upon

The working parent has to be ingenious about getting the load off his back with all kinds of help.

Working parents we know have found help in occasional co-op eating. Good friends invite each other's children for the evening meal—a simple menu like spaghetti and meat balls or chili con carne, bread, salad or vegetable, milk, and fresh fruit—and one set of parents thereby gets some precious time off together. This is badly needed by working parents who are "always under the gun" from one demand or another. It's even more essential when a working parent is carrying a family alone.

Another type of co-op eating includes every member of both families, but it's a kind of covered-dish-supper scheme. One family furnishes the main dish, another the salad, bread and dessert. This eases up the mealtime struggle, and adds that essential ingredient, *fun*, to the meal.

Another co-op idea is to trade frozen dishes with a neighbor. When you're making a casserole, do two. Serve or freeze one for yourself, give the other to your neighbor, and ask him or her to trade off one of theirs to you. This way, both families get more variety and surprise into their meals.

Here's a sneaky ploy. If doting aunts, mothers, grandmas, ask: What kind of gift would you like for your birthday? Christmas? Holidays? Ask for a "food a month" such as a casserole ready-made to pop into the oven for heating. Or a big batch of cookies. Or anything else that would save you cooking and kitchen hassle or give you a night off.

Many families find that food-buying co-ops save time and money and bring better quality food. Is there one in your area? You may find it helpful.

There is no question that the problem of preparing

good, nourishing food by working parents can be relieved in many ways. We hope you'll find this book helpful in making your job at home as efficient as the one you do for a living.

2

Your Kitchen,
Friend or Enemy?

A carefully thought-out kitchen is indispensable to the cooking comfort and efficiency of a working parent.

It can save time, temper, and energy.

Rearranging a kitchen to work for you instead of against you is one of the most useful things a working parent can do to make food preparation much easier and meals more pleasant.

One working parent that we know, Mary Smith,

learned the hard way how important it is to have a kitchen which is a friend instead of an enemy before Mrs. Shell showed her how to rearrange her kitchen.

Mary's kitchen is a simple room with a sink, cupboards, counter space, and refrigerator on one wall; a stove diagonally opposite; a tall cabinet in one corner; and a table and chairs for eating in the opposite corner.

After a hard day at the office, Mary often makes a simple dinner for herself and her three children. The menu is one everybody liked—meat loaf, parslied potatoes, carrots and peas, sliced tomato salad with herb dressing, whole wheat bread, ice cream and oatmeal cookies, milk, and tea.

Before Mary rearranged her kitchen, this is how she made her meat loaf. On arriving home, Mary put on an apron and washed her hands at the sink. She stepped from the sink to the cupboard to the left of it, bent over, and searched the lower cabinet frantically for her meat loaf pan. Four pots fell out on the floor. Finally, after locating the meat loaf pan in the rear of the cabinet, Mary stuffed the pots back into the cabinet and carried the meat loaf pan to the counter between the sink and refrigerator to do her mixing of foods. *Pointer:* A pan should be stored at the area where it will be used first —in this case, in a cupboard beneath or above the mixing area. You save a lot of walking and bending.

Mary next returned to the cupboard at the left of the sink and took out a mixing bowl for her meat loaf and some measuring cups from the cabinet overhead. She took these back to her mixing area. *Pointer:* Mixing bowls and measuring cups should be stored in the same area where the mixing is done.

Mary then opened the refrigerator, removed ground beef and an egg, and placed them in the mixing area. From the cabinet above, she took out salt and pepper.

Next Mary looked for a can of tomato sauce in the same cabinet. Many cans had to be moved around before the tomato sauce was found. *Pointer:* Store canned foods with the most frequently used items in front.

Mary walked to the tall, narrow cabinet on the far wall, took out an onion and a loaf of bread to make bread crumbs, and carried these back to the mixing counter space. *Pointer:* Bread should be stored near the mixing or serving area, or in the refrigerator in summer. Onion should be stored in an open vegetable bin near the sink, but not underneath.

Mary returned to the cupboard at the left of the sink, removed a can opener and mixing spoon from a drawer, and brought them to the mixing area. *Pointer:* Utensils used in assembling recipes should be stored in the mixing area.

Mary took down a chopping board hanging on a well-placed hook on the wall above her mixing area to mince the onion, completed the mixing of the meat loaf, placed it in the pan, and took it to the oven for baking.

You can see that Mary spent more time getting ready to cook than she did cooking. A meat loaf is a very simple dish to make, but Mary's helter-skelter kitchen made it time-consuming and exhausting.

To complete the meal, Mary went over to the cabinet on the far wall of the kitchen, took out potatoes, and brought them to her mixing area. *Pointer:* Potatoes should be stored in an open vegetable bin near but not under the sink, since scrubbing them is the first operation.

Next, to the drawer in the cabinet to the left of the sink for a potato peeler and knife which Mary took to her mixing-area counter. Then back to the cupboard at the left of the sink where, after a lot of rummaging around, a saucepan with cover was located. This was taken to the counter mixing space. Afterward, Mary went to the cupboard to stuff back all the pots that were removed before the saucepan could be located.

Mary then decided to set the table. She opened the cupboard over her mixing area and took from it the dishes needed for dinner, three mugs, and a cup and saucer. From a drawer below, she removed the needed silver. She carried everything to the table to set it. Then the phone rang. Mary escaped gladly for a quick conversation.

Let's leave Mary talking on the telephone instead of following her through every tortuous step of completing her simple meal.

How did Mrs. Shell help Mary to rearrange her kitchen for quick, energy-saving cooking to meet her needs? She began by explaining that everything for cooking should be stored where it is used first. Utensils and equipment then follow cooking actions in a fast, smooth flow. An example of the opposite principle is the thoughtless storage of the meat loaf pan so far from where it was to be used. This resulted in a jerky pattern of movement during the meal preparation with needless, repetitive steps.

Mrs. Shell showed Mary the following scheme of basic work and storage centers for efficient cooking.

Where an individual stores food or utensils will vary according to the kitchen design and type of meals cooked. The scheme that follows is a general guide to placing food and utensils to meet individual needs.

Area 1.   Sink storage-work center (for water and drainage for meal preparation and clean up)

Store foods here that do not need refrigeration, such as dried fruits and vegetables, dried peas and beans, canned foods such as shrimp that need washing before use, canned and dry milk, other canned foods where water is added, fresh potatoes, onions, etc.

Store any utensils to be filled with water, or used with water, such as saucepans for cooking fresh potatoes, coffeepot, large kettle for cooking soups, macaroni, etc. (Covers should be stored at stove, not here.)

Colanders, strainers, funnels, paring knives, peelers, graters, brushes, kitchen scissors, etc., used in cleaning, paring, slicing, chopping or dicing fruits and vegetables; measuring cups for liquids; can and bottle openers.

Dishwashing and cleanup supplies.

Area 2.   Stove storage-work center (provides heat for cooking)

Store foods here that first require boiling water in preparation: teas, instant coffee or other beverage products, hot cereals, all macaroni and pasta products, rice that does not call for rinsing, etc.

Canned vegetables that need no added water for cooking, pepper, salt, other seasonings to add during or at end of cooking.

Store covers for pots, kettles, skillets or fry pans; grid-

dles; some saucepans for heating foods such as pork
and beans which do not need water. Measuring spoons
and cups, slotted spoons, ladles, etc., needed for measuring, stirring, mashing, testing for doneness, turning, carving, and serving from stove.

Additional cutting board for meats and a second can
opener for canned foods.

Area 3. Refrigerator storage-work center (provides for
safekeeping for perishable foods)

Near this storage center, have available refrigerator and
freezer storage containers and covers for fresh and
leftover foods; wraps, aluminum foil; plastic bags;
freezer paper; freezer tape; labels, etc.

Area 4. Mixing storage-work center

Store foods here and other items for mixing and baking
that are always mixed before used: flours, sweeteners,
bought or homemade mixes; fats not requiring refrigeration; salt; leavenings such as baking powder, soda,
dry yeast; spices; herbs; flavorings; salad seasonings;
vinegars; dry milk used as an ingredient, etc.

Utensils and other items needed for mixing: mixing
bowls; beaters; whisks; measuring cups; rolling, grind-
ing and other tools and appliances for doughs, meats,
fruits, vegetables; cutting boards; custard as well as
other baking cups; roasting pans; cookie sheets; cake
and pie pans; casseroles; trivets, etc.

Area 5. Table-service storage center

Storage of food such as ready-to-eat cereals; salt, pepper,
sweeteners; bread, etc.

Dishes, glassware, silverware, napkins, and hot mats for
the table.

This is a good place for trays and a serving cart.

Store electric appliances here for cooking at the table, such as toaster, waffle iron, sandwich maker, etc.

After considering these insights for a kitchen that works *for* people instead of against them, Mary was able to make immediate changes that helped her to cook and serve meals in less time with much less effort. Most of the changes did not cost Mary any money. She shifted bowls, utensils, pans, and frequently used canned and dry foods from other cupboards to her mixing work area. With this change alone, she was able to mix her meat loaf and other recipes in a mere fraction of the time it used to take. Instead of spending time fetching and carrying all the needed items to her mixing area, she put the time into mixing and cooking. She found she was less tired after cooking and began to enjoy making a meal for her family instead of dreading or resenting it.

Having discovered what a difference it made to have an organized storage-work center, Mary decided to spend a little money to set up even more efficient work centers in her kitchen. She bought two good-sized pegboards. She installed one next to the stove to make a stove work center that really functioned, and the other over the sink.

Mary realized that every time she went to the cupboard for a pot or pan, it was clatter, bang and fallout time, and this frayed her temper as well as her efficiency. Using a pegboard next to the stove, she was able to hang most of her skillets, pots, pans, and kitchen tools such as slotted spoons, meat turners, etc., within easy reach of where they were to be used. On Mrs. Shell's advice, Mary placed a narrow table next to the stove at stove height to hold a rack for storing covers for pots, and for setting down pots, pans, spoons, etc., after cooking. Mary found this table in another part of the house. It wasn't getting much use and proved to be perfect for completing her stove work center. Mary is also planning to install a narrow shelf under the pegboard to hold frequently used canned vegetables, sauces, etc., which—with the help of a second can opener hanging on the pegboard—eliminates walking around the kitchen to get food together, opening it, and taking it to the stove.

Mary now set about improving the sink storage center. She installed a pegboard over the sink to hold the potato peeler, vegetable brushes, strainers, colander, measuring cups for liquids, can and bottle opener, and cleanup utensils. This saved many steps formerly used in trotting from drawers, shelves and cupboards to the sink.

Mary is saving her money to buy a storage cabinet to place near her dining table. In this she will store the dishes, mugs, cups and saucers, glasses, silverware for table service, as well as ready-to-eat cereals, some bread, salt, pepper, sweeteners, and napkins. In the lower shelves, she will be able to store foods bought in bulk such as flours, sugar, etc. Smaller quantities of these foods are stored at the mixing center for quick, easy use. This cabinet will also be a good place to store less frequently used equipment, including special appliances such as a waffle iron or turkey roaster pan, etc., to cut down clutter in the rest of this working kitchen.

As suggested, watch your steps, literally, while you go about preparing a meal. Notice where you first use a food or utensil, a bowl or pan. Gradually start shifting these items around to the point where first used, whether the mixing area, stove or sink. Much will depend upon a family's taste and lifestyle. Mary's family, for instance, likes canned peaches chilled for dessert. She stores the peaches in the refrigerator. Other families like canned peaches at room temperature, so they would store them at the table-service storage center. If a family used peaches only in making desserts such as cobblers, puddings, and upside-down cake, the canned peaches would be stored at the mixing area storage center. Where you place both foods and kitchen equipment depends upon how you cook and what you cook.

You may wonder what to do with items not mentioned in the various centers. Simply store them in the center where they are first used, or most frequently used. It is best to store rarely used items in the back of a cabinet or another part of the house where they will not crowd valuable storage space in the kitchen.

As you go about making changes to improve kitchen efficiency, you will find cooking less fatiguing and less time-consuming. Your kitchen will indeed become a friend instead of an enemy.

3

Do Ahead Time

Only yesterday, the families of America grew up in the kitchens of America. People, from the very young to the very old, shared in food preparation while they exchanged news, views, plans and problems. It's time to bring back a bit of that spirit to help working parents.

Do Ahead Time is a modern miniature of that old-fashioned, helpful spirit. In just two hours a week, basic foods can be prepared ahead to make it easier to get meals on working nights when you're tired. Do Ahead

Time makes sure that every day there will be good meals and good nutrition, the keys to high energy and vitality.

But don't be alone in Do Ahead Time. If your kitchen is small, get at least one member of the family to help you. If larger, more can share in the work and the fun. Since working parents have to be away from home so much, Do Ahead Time is an important way to be together, to keep in touch, and for the children to learn a lot of useful things.

In Do Ahead Time, meat for three meals can be prepared in one cooking (see chapter 7, "Accordion Recipes"). At the same time, you may want to put on a robust stew that can be refrigerated for another worry-free working-day meal. Or how about a big pot of hearty soup? These foods cook with little or no watching so other things can be done at the same time.

Is there a favorite family dish too time-consuming to prepare on a work night? Lasagna. Eggplant Parmigiana. A casserole. Let everyone pitch in and help make it while the three-in-one meat is cooking. Freeze it, or refrigerate it, for reheating on a busy workday night. Yes, it's cooking up a storm, but when you get the hang of it, it's a liberating way to live. You're running the show and it feels good. No more dreading dinner time at the end of a working day. No more skimpy take-home meals. No more high cost, ready-to-serve foods.

Use Do Ahead Time, too, to prepare salad greens for a week's meals. Any older child can be taught to take over this task. Fix healthful snacks such as raw carrots and cucumber spears. Prepare and store seasoning vegetables such as onion, celery, green pepper, to use for instant fresh flavor in working-night meals. If rice figures in the week's menus, cook it ahead at this time, and store in the refrigerator for reheating as directed on page 33.

Each working cook will use Do Ahead Time differently. It depends upon the family's favorite meals. Analyze them. See what parts of the work can be done ahead to free you on working nights, and to help avoid the risks of last-minute meals that often run short on nutrition.

How to Prepare and Store Salad Greens

Most people enjoy crisp salads and snapping-fresh raw vegetable snacks. Here's the way to prepare and store them to keep them garden fresh, ready to serve in the week's meals.

First, throw away any bruised parts that are wilted or have insect damage. Wash the salad greens by moving them back and forth in cold water. This will remove any dirt or dust or small insects that may be there. Take the salad greens out of the water and rinse in fresh water a second time. Again take the salad greens out of the water and shake well. Allow them to stand in a strainer or your dish rack until most of the water has run out. Shake to remove any remaining water. Pat dry if necessary.

To store, slightly moisten a clean dish towel, wrap the salad greens in the dish towel, and place in a covered container or a plastic bag. Store in refrigerator. Greens should keep this way for five to seven days, depending upon your refrigerator and how fresh the salad greens were when bought. On busy work nights, salad greens will be all ready to serve, and you won't be tempted to skip this important part of a nutritious and appetizing meal.

Never cut or break up salad greens before storing them. If you do, they will start to spoil, wilt, and become slimy. Cut or break greens only when about to serve them.

Many people store greens unwrapped in the hydrator of the refrigerator. This causes them to wilt and spoil in a very short time.

Salad Greens Variety. Salad greens are so important to health for their vitamins, minerals and roughage that they deserve special attention. Remember, the darker green the leaf, the higher the vitamin A. When nutritionists compared crisp head lettuce such as iceberg with darker greens such as escarole or chicory, they found five times as much vitamin A in equal amounts of these greens as in iceberg lettuce.

Are you familiar with other salad greens besides iceberg lettuce? There's romaine lettuce with long, tapering leaves. There's escarole, a loose-leaved head, white at the base, dark green and ruffled at the tip, with a slight nip to the taste that is very pleasant in a salad. Chicory, or curly endive, as it is sometimes called, is frilly and fancy-looking. It's good by itself and looks delightful in a mixed salad. Then there's Boston lettuce, flat-leaved and loose rather than tightly bunched. Those living near farms may be able to buy field salad, a tender, delicious green with small oval leaves.

Not all these greens may be available where you live but do look for them, learn to recognize them, and enjoy them for their good nutrition and contrasting tastes and textures. If only iceberg lettuce is sold at your market, use it but add vitamin boosters to improve the nutrition of the salad. These might be a few leaves of fresh spinach, some sliced carrot, or some green pepper or watercress. Cooked vitamin A vegetables can be used to boost the iceberg lettuce salad, too, such as peas, green beans, broccoli, and others.

How to Prepare and Store Raw Vegetable Snacks

Carrot Chunks. These are an excellent source of vitamin A but unless they are ready to eat in the refrigerator, your family is not likely to get the benefit of them, or the fun of eating them.

Buy small carrots because they are more tender and better-flavored. Clean the carrots by covering them with cold water and scrubbing them, if needed. Peel or scrape, if desired. Remove tip and base. Cut into small size chunks.

To store, moisten a white paper towel, and wrap carrot chunks in it. Place in a plastic bag or tightly covered container. Store in refrigerator. If the towel dries out, just add a few drops of water to it, rewrap the carrot chunks, and re-store. These chunks should keep for four to five days.

Green Pepper Snacks. When buying green or red peppers, choose firm and fleshy ones. Flabby peppers or those with spots or very thin walls have already started to spoil, and good vitamins have been lost.

Wash peppers, cut in quarters, take out seeds and white part. Pat peppers thoroughly dry. Peppers start to spoil immediately in high humidity. Cut peppers into smaller pieces, if desired.

To store, use same method as for carrots.

Many other vegetables are enjoyable served raw for snacks, and so nutritious. Try zucchini, cauliflowerets, broccoli in small pieces, asparagus cuts, celery stalks, and cucumber spears.

Do Ahead Seasoning Vegetables. It's a great convenience to have chopped onion, diced celery, and strips or slices of green pepper ready to use in the refrigerator for cooking on busy nights. Remember, the thinner the strips of green pepper, the quicker they cook. Store these prepared vegetables in the refrigerator in a tightly covered container with the least amount of air space at the top to avoid drying out. A moist paper towel tucked just inside the cover of the container will help keep vegetables fresh.

If you don't want to invest that much Do Ahead Time chopping and dicing vegetables, try this way of preparing seasoning vegetables. Just peel onions and place in a plastic container with a tight-fitting cover, or in a tightly closed plastic bag, and place in refrigerator until ready to use. When using the onion for cooking, take out the peeled onion and cut it into small pieces, or slice it directly into the cooking pan to save chopping.

For finely chopped or minced onion, cut the onion's surface on all sides until it is scored. Then cut through crosswise until the onion is in very small pieces. Another simple alternative is to rub the peeled onion over the section of a flat hand grater that gives the desired degree of fineness.

As for green pepper, simply wash, cut in half, remove seeds, stem and white part, rinse to remove any remaining seeds, cut in half again, and dry thoroughly. Place in plastic container, cover with moist, not wet, paper towel, close tightly, or store in plastic bag, tightly closed. Refrigerate. For celery, wash and scrub each stalk with a brush to remove sand or grit. Cut away any bruised portion. Dry thoroughly and pack and store as for green pepper. When cooking, slice celery directly into pan.

Cook Ahead Fresh Vegetables

It's a time-saver to cook ahead a double batch of fresh vegetables such as broccoli, green beans, or cauliflower. It's true there is some loss of nutrients as the vegetables stand in the refrigerator and in reheating, but that's better than not having fresh vegetables at all for lack of time to prepare them. Broccoli, green beans and cauliflower can be served hot the first night, and then refrigerated to make a delicious, cold vegetable dish seasoned with French dressing; or they can be heated and served with a simple sauce such as melted butter with lemon or lime juice, or sprinkled with Parmesan cheese, or used in casseroles. *Efficiency tip:* Cook two vegetables at one time with a food steamer placed inside a saucepan.

Do Ahead Cooked Potatoes

It's very handy on busy nights to have cooked potatoes all ready to reheat to make a meal more substantial and nourishing. Heat them as is, or peel and slice into skillet dishes or in quick casserole mixtures. For Do Ahead cooked potatoes, simply scrub potatoes, cook them till done in their skins, and refrigerate until desired.

Baked potatoes may be refrigerated. Slice and pan fry, or butter the slices and place under broiler just long enough to brown tops and heat through.

Do Ahead Bread Crumbs

Soft bread crumbs add a special touch to top-baked dishes or in meat loaf. They give a lighter texture to meat loaf than the commercial variety. To make these bread crumbs, simply crumble fresh bread lightly with your fingers and store in the refrigerator in a tightly covered container or plastic bag with a twist. This is a nice, safe job for a very young child.

Do Ahead Cooked Ground Beef

When you are planning to have two dishes made with ground beef in the same week, such as Sloppy Joes and Chili Con Carne, save time and last-minute cooking by precooking a double batch of ground beef. Refrigerate. Use half for each dish.

Do Ahead Shredded or Chopped Cheese

It's time-consuming and tiring to make shredded cheese at the end of a working day. Prepare it ahead by shredding the cheese with a grater or chopping it fine with a knife. Sprinkle a tablespoon of flour over the prepared cheese and toss lightly. This will keep the cut cheese from sticking together. Refrigerate. The cheese should be stored in the smallest container possible, with a very tight lid, to prevent drying out. Use in a reasonable amount of time as some cheeses develop mold on standing.

Do Ahead Relishes

Relishes add variety, fun and nutrition to a meal. Pickled beets are easy to prepare for the week ahead by just adding vinegar to canned drained beets and refrigerating. Or make a simple corn relish with canned corn seasoned with pickle relish and a small amount of mayonnaise and mustard.

Do Ahead Hard-Cooked Eggs

Do Ahead hard-cooked eggs are an asset in the working parent's kitchen. They can be used for last-minute meals to make up an attractive cold plate, to extend the protein in a meal when you have only a little meat, to use in creamed or curried eggs on rice or toast, to use in casseroles and in salads. Here's how to prepare tender-textured hard-cooked eggs that are easier to peel.

For perfect hard-cooked eggs, buy the eggs five to six days before they are to be used. Store in the refrigerator. Storage allows the eggs' air space at the rounded end of the egg to expand, making it easier to peel off the shell after the egg is cooked.

Eggs to be cooked in the shell should be at room temperature. This takes about two hours after removing them from the refrigerator. To hurry the process, cover the eggs with warm—never hot—water for about twenty minutes. Place them in an enamel saucepan large enough to hold eggs without crowding and allow for adding cold water to at least one inch above the tops of the eggs.

To help prevent cracking of eggs during cooking, puncture eggs before cooking with a sharp needle at the center of the large rounded end. Penetrate only the shell to allow air to escape.

Using high heat, heat only to boiling the water in which the eggs have been placed. Remove from heat at once and cover with a tight-fitting lid. The American Egg Board recommends that the eggs stand in hot water for 15 minutes for large eggs, with the time adjusted by 3 minutes up or down for each size egg larger or smaller. Pour off hot water and cool eggs by running cold water over them. This stops the eggs from cooking, and prevents discoloration. They are easier to peel if this is done immediately. If eggs are not to be eaten at once, it is better to keep them in the shell. Refrigerate until ready to use.

Do Ahead Rice

Cook rice in quantity needed for meals in the week ahead. If rice is cooked in a lot of water, be sure to drain it well before storing. To store, place in a container with a tightly fitting cover and keep in refrigerator.

To reheat rice. *Method 1:* Place cooked rice in food steamer, strainer or colander. Place food steamer, strainer or colander in pan with small amount of water in bottom. Cover, bring to boil, lower heat and simmer until rice is hot. This method fluffs rice as it heats. *Method 2:* This method avoids dishwashing and is quicker but it requires careful watching,which Method 1 does not. Measure out amount of cooked rice needed into a saucepan, add a very small amount of water, cover, heat over very low heat. Remove from heat immediately.

Do Ahead Time can cut out a lot of last-minute fuss when you're tired and rushed at the end of a working day. Choose from these ideas those that fit your cooking preferences to make it easier for you.

4

What Makes a Meal?

What's a good dinner? It tastes good, of course, but a good dinner is more. It's a combination of good-for-you foods, carefully chosen to make a meal high in nutrition. So many dinners fall short of that, then vitality falls short, and doctor bills often increase.

Working parents need to be especially careful to serve dinners high in nutrition because their families often eat outside the home. There is a danger that these meals may be skimpy or not made up of foods needed for good nutrition. A hamburger-on-a-bun lunch, for instance, leaves out vitamin A and vitamin C foods, so necessary to good health.

Our Good Dinner Guide is designed to make up as much as possible for nutrients that may have been missed at lunch and breakfast in the hurried and harried world of the working parent. A good dinner will help take care of nutritional slips and lapses made during the day.

The Good Dinner Guide   2066897

A dinner that is high in nutrition includes:

1 good protein food

1 good vitamin A food, or 2 or more fair sources of vitamin A

1 good vitamin C food, or 2 or more fair sources of vitamin C

1 good iron food, or 2 or more foods that have iron

1 calcium food, preferably milk

1 whole grain food, such as bread

For good health and well-being, it's important to serve this kind of dinner every day, not just once in a while. Sometimes one food is a good source of more than one nutrient and can be used accordingly in meals. Some protein foods such as meats and seafoods are good sources of both protein and iron. In this case, a separate iron food will not be needed. Broccoli is high in both vitamin A and vitamin C. It's a two-in-one vitamin food that eliminates the need for serving either a vitamin A or vitamin C food separately. But this is rare.

How is a person to know which foods are sources of each nutrient, such as vitamins, minerals, protein? The chart Foods Needed Every Day, pages 40–41, sums it up, easy as ABC. Use it for a quick guide to building meals that include all the nutrients needed. The listings of food sources of each nutrient at the end of the book make it easy to put together foods in good nutritional combinations.

If you follow our menus exactly, you will shift automatically to higher nutrition because each menu has been planned to bring you all the nutrients needed at one meal. Each is a well-balanced package of protein, vitamins, minerals, and other nutrients. When your taste preferences indicate substitutions, be sure to consult the charts to choose a food that is a good alternate in nutrition to the disliked one omitted from the menu.

Nutrition Is No Mystique

Now let's take the mystique out of making nourishing meals. Good nutrition is neither complicated nor fancy. This menu for a high-nutrition meal will be familiar to most people. The carrots and potatoes are cooked in one pot to cut down dishwashing and conserve vitamins.

Hamburger Patties with Pepper Relish
Carrots and Potatoes
Tomato Slices
Whole Wheat Bread and Spread
Pineapple Chunks
Milk
Tea or Coffee, if desired

What is the nutrition pedigree of this simple meal? Hamburger and milk are both good protein foods. The hamburger also adds iron to the meal, and the milk adds calcium and riboflavin in addition to its complete protein. The carrots contribute vitamin A. There is vitamin C in both the potatoes and the tomatoes which, taken together, add up to a good source, and the pineapple has a small amount of C, too. The whole wheat bread adds thiamine, riboflavin, niacin and iron besides fiber to this high-nutrition meal.

Now let's take a high-nutrition meal that has no meat.

Homemade Macaroni and Cheese
Broccoli   Pickled Beets
Whole Wheat Bread with Spread
Easy-Do Prunes and Apricots
Milk
Tea or Coffee, if desired

In this meal, the Macaroni and Cheese and the milk furnish complete protein. The enriched macaroni has incomplete protein, but it is improved in quality by the cheese and milk in the meal, both of which are complete protein foods. The broccoli, as previously mentioned, is high in both vitamin A and vitamin C. Macaroni and cheese is not rich in iron. However, the combination of foods in this menu was carefully chosen to add up to about 35 percent of the iron needs for the day for an average person. Even the dessert of Easy-Do Prunes and Apricots contributes iron to the meal.

As for the beets, they have only very small amounts of some of the basic nutrients. However, they are flavorful, colorful, low in calories, and give pleasant contrast in texture. In this menu, where broccoli has already provided the needed vitamin A and vitamin C, beets are an acceptable choice, and this applies in any menu where a single vegetable or fruit, or other food, provides sufficient vitamin A and C.

Now for a look at the iron content of beets. It is commonly believed that beets are high in iron but this is not true. A half cup of diced or sliced, cooked beets gives only 2 percent of the daily iron requirement. However, the beet greens which are often discarded have a different story. A half cup of cooked beet greens gives about 8 percent of the iron needed daily as well as 75 percent of the daily requirement of vitamin A and about 15 percent of the vitamin C. Compare the iron content of beet greens with canned baked beans of which a half-cup serving gives about 15 percent of the daily iron need. Another comparison is with an average serving of beef liver, which gives in one food about 40 percent of the iron needed daily. It's important to know that in complete protein foods, iron is used more efficiently by the body than the iron from plant sources, including grains. This is one demonstration of why it is so important to choose a variety of foods when planning a day's meals.

Both the enriched macaroni and the whole wheat bread in this meal provide some thiamine, riboflavin, niacin and iron in inexpensive form. The milk contributes protein, calcium and riboflavin. Thus a meal high in all the nutrients is rounded out with a careful selection of foods.

In our menus, bread and milk is included to round out the meal to be nutritionally adequate. When you include bread and milk in your menus, you can use less of the expensive high-protein foods. For instance, you need only 2 ounces of cooked ham in a main dish when you serve milk with the meal because, together, the two foods have all the protein you need at one meal.

When dinner is regarded in this light, meal preparation becomes clearly a lot more than shopping and cooking. If meals are planned for good nutrition as well as good taste, the family's well-being and enjoyment of life are greatly increased.

You may also be interested in the chart Key Nutrients, pages 172–175, which outlines the role nutrients perform in the body: for example, vitamin A helps to keep the skin and inner linings of the body healthy and resistant to infection, while calcium helps to build bones, aids blood-clotting, and helps nerves and muscles to react normally.

Use the handy guide, Foods Needed Every Day, to help plan more nutrition into meals served at home.

FOODS NEEDED EVERY DAY

Fruit and Vegetable Group   4 or more servings as follows

1 serving is 1/2 cup fruit, vegetable, or juice or 1 medium piece of fruit.

Important Nutrient Supplied	*Food Sources*
Vitamin C (ascorbic acid) plus other vitamins. 1 or more serving each day	Citrus fruit or juice, such as orange, grapefruit, tangerine, or lemon; fresh strawberries; cantaloupe; or such vegetables as tomatoes, broccoli, cabbage, dark green leafy vegetables, peppers, and potatoes.
Vitamin A (from carotene in food which is converted by the body to vitamin A) plus other vitamins and minerals. 1 or more serving each day	Dark green or deep yellow vegetable or fruit, such as broccoli, apricots, cantaloupe, carrots, chard, collards, cress, kale, mango, persimmon, pumpkin, spinach, sweet potato, turnip greens, winter squash.
Vitamins, minerals and carbohydrates. 2 or more servings each day	Additional vegetables high in vitamin A or C; as well as other vegetables, such as corn, beets, mushrooms, eggplant, onions, etc.

Grain Group   4 or more servings each day

1 serving is 1 slice of bread or 1 ounce of cereal

Important Nutrient Supplied	*Food Sources*
Thiamine, riboflavin, iron, niacin, incomplete protein, other vitamins, minerals, carbohydrate and cellulose (fiber, bulk or roughage).	Preferably whole-grain breads and cereals; or enriched or restored. Includes: bread; cereals such as rolled oats and farina; and unsweetened ready-to-eat cereals, such as shredded wheat; brown or enriched rice; noodles; macaroni; grits; and cornmeal.

Protein Group   2 or more servings each day

1 serving is 2–3 ounces cooked lean meat, fish, chicken. 1/2 serving is 1 egg; 1/2 cup cooked dry beans, dry peas or lentils; or 2 tablespoons peanut butter.

Important Nutrient Supplied	*Food Sources*
Complete protein, iron, B vitamins (niacin, thiamine, riboflavin), plus other minerals and vitamins.	Eggs, cheese, milk, fish, meats (beef, veal, pork, lamb, game), poultry. Dried beans, peas, peanut butter, and nuts as alternates when served with small amounts of complete protein food.

Milk Group   2 or more servings each day

1 serving is 1 cup: Children under 9 need 2–3 cups; children 9–12, 3 or more cups; teenagers, 4 or more cups; adults, 2 or more cups; pregnant women, 3 or more cups; nursing mothers, 4 or more cups.

Calcium, phosphorus, riboflavin, vitamin A, and protein.	Milk, or equivalent in calcium: 1-inch cube Cheddar cheese = 1/2 cup milk; 1/2 cup cottage cheese = 1/3 cup milk; 2 tablespoons cream cheese = 1 tablespoon milk; 1/2 cup ice cream or ice milk = 1/4 cup milk.
Vitamin D when milk is fortified with D.	

Other Foods Group   According to energy need

Fat: Some provide vitamin A and essential fatty acids.	Butter, margarine, cooking fat, lard, and oils, fish liver oil, salad oil, bacon, fat in meats, peanut butter, cream, nuts, mayonnaise, chocolate and avocado.
Sweeteners: Carbohydrates, mainly calories from sugar.	Sugars, jelly, honey, molasses, etc.

About 1,500 calories are furnished by the minimum number of servings recommended. To meet individual needs, add more from the above groups plus moderate amounts of fat and limited amounts of sweeteners. Children 1–10 need 1300–2400 calories, males 11 up, 2400–3000 calories, females 11 up 1800–2400 calories. Specific needs depend upon age, size, and activity.

What's a Good Lunch?

A good lunch takes care of from one-fourth to one-third of the calorie needs for the day. It provides enough food to prevent a midafternoon drop in blood sugar, or that hollow feeling. This often leads to snacking on foods low in nutrition and high in calories, such as doughnuts and cakes. Sometimes the result is overweight and lowered well-being.

A lunch that is high in nutrition includes:

1 protein food

1 grain food

1 fruit or vegetable or both

Milk or a food made from milk such as cheese

There are many choices to make within this range of foods for midday meals high in nutrition. Here are examples to suit many tastes and to fit any budget of time or money. Most of these lunches can also be toted to work or school. Pack properly to avoid risk of food spoilage.

Good-Nutrition Sandwich Lunches

Cheddar or Swiss Cheese Sandwich
Coleslaw
Plums
Coffee or tea

No milk to drink is needed with
this lunch because it includes
natural cheese, a food made from milk.

Fish Sandwich
Raw Spinach Salad
An Orange
Milk
Coffee or Tea

Egg Sandwich
Tomato Salad
A Pear
Milk
Coffee or Tea

To reduce calories, slice hard-cooked egg over tomato salad; use one slice of bread instead of two; use skim milk.

Chicken Sandwich
Raw Carrot and Green Pepper Chunks
Banana
Milk
Coffee or Tea

Peanut Butter Sandwich
Carrot and Raisin Salad
Orange or Grapefruit
Milk
Coffee or Tea

Milk is necessary with this meal to improve the quality of incomplete protein in the peanut butter.

Tomato Juice
Cottage Cheese-Fruit Spread
on Nutbread Sandwich
Milk
Coffee or Tea

Good-Nutrition Soup Lunches

Split Pea or Bean Soup
Cheese and Crusty Bread
An Apple
Milk
Coffee or Tea

*The complete protein in the cheese
and milk improves the incomplete
protein in the soup.*

Vegetable Beef Soup
Mixed Green Salad with Egg Slices
Bread
Grapes
Milk
Coffee or Tea

Good-Nutrition Plate Lunches

Cottage Cheese with Chopped Fruit
on Greens with Yogurt Dressing
Nutbread
Milk
Coffee or Tea

Tuna or Chicken Salad
Sliced Tomatoes
Green Pepper Rings
Oatmeal Bread
A Peach
Milk
Coffee or Tea

Good-Nutrition Yogurt Lunch

Big Serving of Strawberries
with Plain Yogurt
Date-Nut Bread (2 slices)
Coffee or Tea

*A container of yogurt does not make
a good lunch in itself; it's a good
start.*

Drinking a cup of milk with most luncheon meals makes budget sense as well as nutrition sense. Milk is a lot of nutrition for the money. Look at it this way. One cup of milk provides 20 percent of the protein needed for a day. Therefore, the amount of more expensive protein foods such as meat, fish and chicken can be cut down in the meal. This is a real money saver. A cup of milk also provides 25 percent of the riboflavin and 30 percent of the calcium needed each day as well as 6 percent of the vitamin A and 4 percent of the vitamin C and thiamine. For busy families on the run, milk is protection for helping to make sure there's good nutrition in every meal.

When shopping for milk, be sure to check labels. Some milk on the market sells at a lower price because vitamin D (essential to good nutrition) has not been added.

What's a Good Breakfast?

A good breakfast is one that takes care of about one-fourth of the calorie needs for the day. Like a good lunch, it prevents the perils of snacking. People who have a good breakfast generally don't feel the need for more food at 10 AM.

A high-nutrition breakfast includes:

   1 fruit, or fruit or vegetable juice

   1 hot or cold (non-sweetened) cereal with milk or 1 egg or other protein food

   Bread with margarine or butter

   Milk to drink

For those who find a cereal or egg breakfast boring, or dislike these foods, there are plenty of other high-nutrition foods to eat in the morning. Here are some non-traditional breakfasts that do not call for any cooking and are quick to prepare.

Tomato Juice
Cheese Sandwich
Milk
Coffee or Tea

Ricotta Cheese with Cinnamon
and Sliced Bananas
Apricot-Nut Bread
Milk
Coffee or Tea

Cottage Cheese with Peaches
Raisin Bread Toast
Milk
Coffee or Tea

Strawberries
Plain Yogurt
Whole Wheat Toast
Coffee or Tea

Sliced Bananas with Milk
Pineapple–Peanut Butter Sandwich
Milk
Coffee or Tea

On mornings when there is more time to prepare breakfast, milk, egg and flour can be combined to make waffles or pancakes, or bread, milk and egg used to make French toast.

Divide and Conquer

People who find a regular, high-nutrition breakfast too much food at one meal can divide it into two smaller meals. A breakfast of an orange, bran flakes with milk, rye bread with cottage cheese spread, milk and coffee, can be divided as follows:

7:00 AM	An Orange Bran Flakes with Milk Coffee or Tea
10:00 AM	Bread and spread Milk

A Heartier Breakfast

A heavier breakfast may be needed for very active people. In this case, add an egg to the breakfast of fruit, cereal with milk, bread and spread, with milk to drink, and coffee or tea. For an even more substantial breakfast, add more bread or some potatoes.

The Buzz-Up Breakfast

On mornings when time is short, try this blender breakfast:

Blender Breakfast Drink
Whole Wheat Toast and Spread
Coffee or Tea, if desired

For the Blender Breakfast Drink, just blend three-fourths cup milk, one-fourth cup orange juice, small banana, dash cinnamon, and a few drops of vanilla extract in an electric blender. This makes a high-nutrition breakfast in a beverage when served with whole wheat bread. To make a more substantial breakfast in a beverage, add an egg when blending the milk mixture.

Other Protein Foods for Breakfast

Leftovers, such as macaroni and cheese, noodle or bread pudding, chili, baked beans and ham, etc., make good protein foods for breakfast in place of cereal or eggs. Thick buttermilk may be served instead of yogurt.

To cut down on the amount of fat at breakfast, use cottage cheese as a spread for bread in place of butter or margarine, and serve skim milk in place of regular milk.

Above all, do enjoy a high-nutrition breakfast each morning. It's a passport to well-being for the day. Complete the "nutrition trip" with a good lunch and dinner.

5

Just for Fathers

Fathers living in households separate from their children sometimes have a problem feeding the kids when they come over to stay. These men usually have high expenses supporting two households, and there may not be much money left for eating out. They face another problem: They don't want to have a relationship with their children based only on entertaining them. Put the two problems together, and you get the perfect solution. Let the kids help get together very simple, good meals at home that everyone will enjoy.

This doesn't mean drudgery. It's really fun. A father told us how his two young sons help him to make a favorite dinner when they come to spend the weekend. They make stuffed roast chicken. The eight-year-old fixes the simple stuffing. It may be just liquefying a packaged mix. The younger son stuffs it "into the chicken's tushi." Baking potatoes are put on at the same time as the chicken. The oven is set at a low temperature, and everybody goes out to the ball park or to swim in the pool. Two hours later, dinner is ready to serve except for some sliced tomatoes and a frozen vegetable. Add milk to drink, and a delicious, nourishing meal is shared by all.

Cleaning up the kitchen together is family sharing, too, and then it's time for favorite TV programs, games, or reading, and a relaxing evening with Dad.

Dinner can require even less effort to prepare and still be a good-tasting, nourishing meal. Stick a chicken in the oven, whole or quartered, to slow-bake to juicy tenderness. No stuffing needed. Locate a store that sells good, fresh potato salad and coleslaw. Serve these with the chicken along with some crusty bread. That's a fine meal, too. It's far cheaper than eating out and much cozier.

In chapter 6, "Quick and Easy Recipes," and in chapter 8, "Throw Together Meals," fathers will find very easy main dishes for serving to children, even if they have never cooked before. Since menus are given in many cases, it isn't difficult to figure out what to add to make a meal high in nutrition and eating satisfaction.

Children especially like One-Pot Macaroni and

Cheese, One-Pot Spanish Rice, and One-Pot Beef and Macaroni made with tomato sauce. These are easy main dishes that require very few ingredients and the minimum of equipment. All the Throw Together Meals are suitable for children, with the possible exception of the celebration seafood meal. This may be too rich for some youngsters but not for others.

Breakfast at Home

Fathers report that breakfast raises problems when children sleep over. Often tired, fathers don't feel like leaping out of bed to go out to breakfast. Children, preferring to lie around in their pajamas, are reluctant to wash and dress as soon as they rise. A good solution to this problem is to plan for breakfast the night before, with everybody understanding where it is, whether cupboard, counter top, or refrigerator. Then each one can get up when he wishes, serve himself, and let Dad have the rest he needs. Be sure to have the children help with preparations the night before. It's part of being a family.

Set the breakfast table before going to bed with plastic glasses, silverware, napkins. Most of the food will be on plates in the refrigerator, in bowls on the counter top, or set at each person's place at the table.

Here are some easy breakfast menus and plans.

Tomato Juice
Cheese Sandwich
Banana

Have tomato juice ready to pour in refrigerator. Make cheese sandwiches; wrap in waxed paper or plastic wrap and place on plate in refrigerator. Put bananas on counter top or at table. Children pour juice next morning, or if too young for that, leave juice in individual plastic tumblers in refrigerator, covered at top with plastic wrap. They unwrap their cheese sandwiches, as much fun as a picnic, and eat their banana out of hand. Milk can be served with this meal, but it isn't necessary nutritionally because the cheese has the same complete protein and other nutrients.

Orange
Ham Sandwich
Milk

Cut orange in quarters, and wrap tightly in plastic wrap. Make ham sandwiches, wrap, and store in refrigerator. Have milk ready, to be poured at breakfast.

Canned Sliced Peaches
Topped with
Container of Yogurt
Slice of Raisin Bread
Milk

For each person, place canned peaches and yogurt in a bowl, cover with plastic wrap and store in refrigerator. Have raisin bread on counter. In morning, everyone helps himself; toast bread, if children are old enough to use toaster, or eat without toasting, or leave individually wrapped slices of store-bought banana bread for breakfasters. For additional suggestions, see breakfast menus in chapter 4.

Your Food Bank

What are some foods you can keep on hand ready to eat that require no cooking? Bread. Milk. Juices such as orange, tomato, pineapple, apple. Cheese. Most children like Swiss, Cheddar, and cottage cheese. Fresh or canned fruit. Moderate amounts of take-in sliced roast beef or boiled ham. Canned tuna or other canned fish. Canned baked beans. Yogurt. Ready-to-eat cereals. Fresh vegetables that can be eaten raw such as cherry tomatoes, celery stalks, carrot chunks, zucchini slices, cucumber spears, watercress sprigs, etc. Also keep on hand graham crackers, fruit bars, oatmeal cookies, and ice cream.

Fruit is fun to eat out of hand, or try these ideas. Instead of cutting cantaloupe or other melon in wedges, try cutting the melon in circles, taking out seeds and peeling it. In the center of each slice, place a scoop of ice cream. For three people or more, try Add-a-Fruit Salad or Fruit Cup. One person slices banana into each person's bowl. Another adds a few slices of canned peaches, and another adds four or five grapes. This gives you a chance to stay out of the kitchen, and everybody shares in the fun.

With a can of tuna or other fish on hand, you can always make up a quick, nourishing meal with a scoop of tuna, sliced tomatoes, a slice of bread, heated baked beans, milk and fruit.

Eating Out—Helps and Hints

Many parents report that when children eat out, they get confused, don't behave well, and are reluctant to eat a nourishing meal. When you do take the children out for dinner, try this plan. Offer them a choice of either chicken or a hamburger pattie instead of reading from a long list of entrées. The father makes a bargain that he will order the rest of the meal, and they'll all eat the same thing. This affords a chance to put together a really nourishing meal with accompaniments to the meat such as baked potato, carrots or other nutritious vegetable, coleslaw and milk to drink. If they want dessert, offer a choice of ice cream or baked apple, and avoid all junk sweets.

When taking the children to fast-food places or a pizza parlor, play the Before and After Game. Have some food before going and some afterward at home. This insures a nourishing meal that is sometimes diffi-cult to obtain outside the home. Before leaving, serve finger foods such as carrot chunks or green pepper rings, and tomato juice. Then go for the hamburger on a bun, or to the pizza parlor. Now back home for milk with fruit, ice cream, or pudding for dessert.

If the kids give you flak for too many french fries, make a bargain that you'll get one order and everyone will share it. French fries are potatoes cooked in a lot of fat, which fill a child up too quickly, leaving insufficient room for necessary nutritious foods. Children often waste an order of french fries, if one is ordered for each. Try ordering less and see how it works.

Alternates to Eating Lunch Out

Lunch is often part of the fun of spending a day out with Dad. However, if you'd rather eat at home, here are a couple of alternates. Serve a lunch of slices of cheese on good bread with cherry tomatoes and watercress sprigs, a glass of milk, with fresh fruit and cookies for dessert. If you want to take a little more time to make the cheese and bread extra special, run the cheese-covered bread under the broiler until the cheese becomes hot and bubbly. It happens quickly, so watch carefully.

A cold combination makes a quick, nourishing lunch. Put a scoop of cottage cheese in a bowl. Top with sliced peaches, bananas and grapes. Serve a bought nut or fruit bread as dessert along with a glass of milk.

It's often surprising that when you are rushing to a matinee or ball game with the children, a quick lunch at home takes less time than waiting in line at a fast-food place.

We hope these ideas will make it easier for fathers and children to enjoy a more relaxed family life together.

6
Quick and Easy Recipes

Surprise.

That was the reaction of the working parents who tested these recipes for us: surprise at how easy the recipes looked, surprise at how good the dishes tasted after so little work, and surprise at the tiny amount of cleanup after cooking, often no more than one pot, a measuring cup, and a paring knife.

It was amusing to watch people with these recipes. They seldom realized that the dish was ready to serve after so little effort, and stood rereading the recipe, feeling that they must have overlooked some steps in the process because they couldn't be finished so easily. We think you will find these recipes a new experience in cooking. They should ease life considerably at the end of a working day.

Because working parents cook for children, who often have conservative tastes, ingredients and seasonings have been kept bland and gentle. But these recipes were designed to season as you please with your favorite herbs, spices, or other flavorings. They are basic recipes to adapt in flavor as you like.

In the recipes that call for a pot or fry pan with a tight-fitting cover, simmering is essential to success. In fact, if you see steam come clouding out, it's a sign that the heat is too high and should be lowered at once. Equipment and gadgets are kept to a minimum. The terms skillet and fry pan are used interchangeably.

The recipes that follow are real family food, not fancy, but full of good, natural flavor and eating satisfaction. These are hearty main dishes that won't leave you feeling hollow an hour or two after dinner.

One-Pot Macaroni and Cheese

Makes 4 servings

3	cups water
1	small onion, chopped, or 1/2 cup Do Ahead chopped onion
1	teaspoon salt
1	teaspoon dry mustard
4	drops bottled hot pepper sauce, if desired
1/2	pound (2 cups) uncooked elbow macaroni
1/3	cup milk
1/2	pound cheddar cheese, shredded (2 cups) or cut into small pieces
	Paprika, if desired

Measure the *water, onion, salt, dry mustard* and *hot pepper sauce* into a 4-quart Dutch oven or other large pot with a tight-fitting cover. Bring to a boil on top of the stove.

Gradually add the macaroni and stir it into the boiling water so that the water continues to boil. Stir to separate macaroni.

Cover. Reduce heat and simmer (keep below a boil but still moving) until macaroni is tender and almost all the liquid is absorbed, about 12 minutes. Stir occasionally to prevent macaroni from sticking to pot.

Stir in *milk* until well blended with macaroni. Cook over low heat for 1 minute.

Gently stir in shredded *cheese* while stirring and mixing only until cheese is melted. Do not boil.

Taste. Stir in additional seasonings, if needed. Serve immediately. Sprinkle with paprika.

Beef and Macaroni in a Pot

Makes 4 servings

1	pound lean ground beef
2	cups (16 ounces) tomato sauce
2 2/3	cups water
1	teaspoon salt
2	cups (8 ounces) uncooked elbow macaroni

Grated cheese, if desired

Place the *ground beef* in an unheated 4-quart Dutch oven or 12-inch fry pan with a tight-fitting cover. Brown the beef. Stir frequently to break up meat and prevent sticking. Fat for browning is not usually needed because there is some fat in the ground beef. Should the beef give off fat, spoon off and discard.

Add the *tomato sauce, water,* and *salt* to browned beef. Stir until well mixed. Cover. Bring to a rapid, full rolling boil.

Gradually add and stir the *macaroni* into the boiling water so water continues to boil. Stir to separate macaroni. Cover. Reduce heat. Simmer (keep water below a boil but still moving) over low heat for 15 minutes or until macaroni is tender. Stir occasionally to prevent sticking.

Serve immediately. Sprinkle with grated cheese.

VARIATIONS

Change flavor of this recipe by adding one of the following when you are adding the salt, in the amounts suggested, or in amounts to suit your taste.

- Oregano   1/2 teaspoon
- Chili powder   1 teaspoon
- Fresh parsley, chopped   3 tablespoons
- Carrot, grated   1/4 cup
- Green olives, sliced   2–3 tablespoons

One-Pot Spanish Rice

Makes 4 servings

>3/4   pound lean ground beef
>1   medium onion, chopped
>1/2   cup chopped green pepper
>
>2   cups (16 ounces) undrained canned tomatoes
>3   cups water
>1   cup uncooked rice
>1   teaspoon salt
>1/2   teaspoon Worcestershire sauce
>
>Additional salt if needed

Place chopped *beef, onions,* and *green pepper* in a 4-quart Dutch oven or other large pot with a tight-fitting cover. Cook over medium heat until beef is browned, and onion and pepper are tender. Spoon off and discard fat given off by beef.

Stir in *tomatoes, water, rice, salt* and *Worcestershire sauce.* Mix well to break up meat. Bring to a boil. Stir and mix well. Cover. Reduce heat. Simmer (keep liquid below a boil but still moving) about 30 minutes or until rice is tender and most of the liquid is absorbed. Stir occasionally to prevent sticking. Add additional water if needed.

Taste. Add additional seasoning if needed.

One-Pot Spaghetti Beef Stroganoff

Makes 4 servings

1	pound lean ground beef
1	small onion, chopped, or 1/2 cup chopped Do Ahead onions
4	cups water
1	teaspoon salt
1	teaspoon dry mustard
	Black pepper to taste
4	drops bottled hot pepper sauce
1/2	pound (8 ounces) uncooked spaghetti, broken into pieces
1	cup or 8-ounce container sour cream or yogurt, more if wanted
	Paprika

Place the *ground beef* and *chopped onion* in an unheated 4-quart Dutch oven or other large pot with a tight-fitting cover. Brown the beef. Stir frequently to break up meat and prevent sticking. Fat for browning is not usually needed because there is some fat in the ground beef. Should the beef give off fat, spoon it off and discard.

Add the *water, salt, dry mustard, black pepper,* and *hot pepper sauce.* Cover. Bring to a rapid, full, rolling boil.

Gradually add and stir the *spaghetti* into the boiling water so water continues to boil. Stir to separate spaghetti. Cover. Lower heat. Simmer (keep water below a boil but still moving) over low heat for 20 minutes or until spaghetti is tender and almost all the liquid is absorbed. Stir occasionally to prevent spaghetti from sticking to pot.

Stir in *sour cream.* Gently stir and mix for about 2 minutes or just until mixture is heated thoroughly. Do not boil.

Serve immediately. Sprinkle with *paprika.*

•

One-Pot Tomato Chicken with Green Peas

Makes 4 servings

2 1/2 to 3   pound chicken, cut into serving pieces (chicken cooks faster when thigh is cut from drumstick, wing from breast, and breast cut in half)

1   can (1 pound) tomatoes or tomato sauce

1   onion, sliced or cut into pieces

1/2   teaspoon oregano or tarragon, more or less, to taste
Salt and pepper to taste

1 to 2   packages (10 ounces each) frozen peas or 1/2 to 1 bag (20 ounces) peas, enough for family needs

Place the cut-up *chicken* in an unheated 4-quart Dutch oven or other large pot with a tight-fitting cover. Pour *canned tomatoes* over chicken. Mash or cut tomatoes when they are whole. Add cut-up *onion.* Cover. Bring to a boil. Lower heat and simmer (keep liquid below a boil but still moving) for 25 minutes or until chicken is almost done.

Stir in *oregano* or *tarragon* (or other favorite herb), *salt, pepper,* and *peas.* Cover. Cook 8 to 10 minutes or until peas are just tender. Do not overcook.

Taste. Add more seasoning, if needed.

VARIATIONS

- Use frozen broccoli or mixed vegetables in place of peas.
- Do Ahead cooked potatoes may be sliced and added to the pot during the last five minutes of cooking time.

MENU SUGGESTION

Serve with noodles or steamed potatoes, carrot chunks, bread, applesauce, milk, and coffee or tea.

●

Main Dish Chicken Soup

Makes 4 servings

2 1/2 to 3   pound chicken, cut into serving pieces
                 (chicken cooks faster when thigh is
                 cut from drumstick, wing from breast,
                 and breast cut in half)
        1   onion, thinly sliced
        1   cup raw regular rice (not instant)
      1/2   teaspoon tarragon leaves, if desired
        5   cups water

        1   package (10-ounce) frozen mixed
                 vegetables
            Salt to taste

Place the cut-up *chicken* in a 4-quart Dutch oven or other large pot with a tight-fitting cover. Add the *sliced onion, raw rice, tarragon leaves* and *water*. Bring to a boil. Lower heat. Cover. Simmer (keep water below a boil but still moving) 30 minutes, or until chicken is almost done.

Add *mixed vegetables* and *salt* to taste. Cover. Simmer until vegetables are cooked, about 8 to 10 minutes.

One-Pot Chili Con Carne

Makes 4 servings

1	pound lean ground beef
2	medium onions, chopped
1 to 3	teaspoons chili powder
2	cups (16 ounces) tomato sauce
1	can (20-ounce) undrained kidney beans
1	teaspoon salt

Place *ground beef* and *onion* in a large skillet with tight-fitting cover. Brown meat over medium low heat. Stir frequently to break up meat and prevent sticking. Fat for browning is not usually needed because there is some fat in the ground beef. Should beef give off fat, spoon it off and discard.

Stir in *chili powder, tomato sauce, kidney beans,* and *salt.* Bring to a boil. Cover. Lower heat and simmer (keep below a boil but still moving) for 20 to 30 minutes.

MENU SUGGESTION

Serve with rice, green leafy vegetable, celery sticks, crunchy bread, a pear, milk, and coffee or tea.

Quickie "Cassoulet"
(Sausage and Beans in a Pot)

Makes 4 servings

3/4	pound raw sausage, cut into 1 1/2 inch pieces
1/2	cup water
1	can (1 pound 4 ounces) fully cooked, undrained white kidney beans
1 to 2	packages (10-ounce) frozen green beans, or 1/2 to 1 bag (20-ounce size) frozen green beans
1/4 to 1/2	teaspoon tarragon, oregano, cumin, or red crushed pepper
	Salt and pepper to taste

Place the cut-up *sausage* in medium-size skillet or Dutch oven. Add *water.* Cover. Cook over medium low heat for 5 minutes or until the sausage loses its pink-red color. Remove cover and cook sausage until browned. Turn to brown evenly. Spoon off and discard all but 1 tablespoon of fat in pan.

Stir in *canned beans.* Cover and cook over low heat for 5 minutes. Stir to prevent sticking. Mixture should be the consistency of a thick creamy soup. If needed, add 1/4 cup or more water.

Add amount of frozen *green beans* to meet your family needs. Sprinkle with spice or herb of your choice. Stir to mix well. Cover. Cook over medium low heat until green beans are cooked. Stir occasionally to prevent sticking.

When vegetables are cooked, taste and add *salt* and *pepper,* if needed.

VARIATION

● Use fresh spinach in place of green beans.

●

Savory Tuna Scallop

Makes 4 servings

1/2	teaspoon salt
1/4 to 1/2	teaspoon poultry seasoning
	Black pepper to taste
1/2	teaspoon Worcestershire sauce
2	medium-size eggs
1	can (6 1/2 to 7 ounces) tuna and oil, flaked
1	cup cottage cheese
1/4	cup dry bread or cracker crumbs
1/2	cup soft bread crumbs
2	tablespoons butter or margarine

Measure the *salt, poultry seasoning, pepper,* and *Worcestershire sauce* into a bowl. Add *eggs* and mix with seasonings until well blended.

Stir in *flaked tuna with oil, cottage cheese,* and *dry bread* or *cracker crumbs.* Mix and stir until well blended. Spoon tuna mixture into a greased, 1-quart casserole.

Arrange *soft bread crumbs* over tuna mixture and dot with *butter or margarine.*

Set in a pan of hot water. Bake in a preheated 375° F. oven for about 35 minutes or until set. Serve immediately.

MENU SUGGESTION

Serve with broccoli, potatoes, celery and tomato salad, oatmeal bread, fresh fruit, milk, and coffee or tea.

Ham and Corn Casserole

Makes 4 servings

2	tablespoons butter or margarine
1/4	cup finely chopped green pepper
2	tablespoons chopped onion
1	can (1 pound 1 ounce) cream-style corn
1/2	cup cracker or dry bread crumbs
1/2	cup milk
3/4	teaspoon salt
	Pepper to taste
2	cups cut-up canned, boiled or home-cooked ham
	Additional cracker or bread crumbs (about 1/4 cup)
	Paprika

Melt *butter* or *margarine* in a medium-size saucepan.

Add *green pepper* and *onion*. Cook, stirring occasionally, until tender. Do not brown.

Stir in *corn*, 1/2 cup *crumbs, milk, salt* and *pepper*. Cook for 5 minutes, stirring occasionally.

Stir *ham* into corn mixture.

Pour into greased 1 1/2-quart baking dish or casserole. Sprinkle top with *bread* or *cracker crumbs* and *paprika*.

Bake in a preheated 350° F. oven for 20 minutes or until hot and bubbly.

MENU SUGGESTION

Ham and Corn Casserole, carrots, coleslaw, pumpernickel bread, fresh fruit, milk, and coffee or tea.

No Hassle Baked Fish

Makes 4 servings

- 1/3   cup butter or margarine
- 3/4   cup fresh soft bread crumbs
- 3/4   cup cracker crumbs

- 1   pound fish fillets (such as cod or other white fish) or scallops
  Salt and pepper to taste

- 2/3   cup milk or cream

Melt *butter* or *margarine* in a saucepan. Stir in *bread* and *cracker crumbs*. Gently stir and toss until melted fat is evenly distributed in crumbs.

Spread half the buttered crumbs in the bottom of a shallow 9-inch baking dish.

Arrange cut-up *fish* or *scallops* in a single layer over the crumbs. *Salt* and *pepper* to taste.

Top with remaining buttered crumbs.

Pour *milk* over crumbs so they are evenly moistened.

Bake in preheated 350° F. oven for 30 minutes, or until done.

MENU SUGGESTION

Serve with scalloped tomatoes (baked along with the fish), broccoli, cucumber spears, bread, strawberries, milk, and coffee or tea.

Skillet Pork Chops

Makes 4 servings

1	tablespoon butter or margarine
1 to 1 1/4	pounds thinly sliced pork chops, less than 1/2-inch thick
1	green pepper, cut into thin slices
1	cup (8 ounces) canned or homemade tomato sauce
1	can (4-ounce) mushrooms, well drained
3 to 4	medium-size cooked (Do Ahead) potatoes, sliced
	Salt and pepper to taste
	Herbs of your choice

Melt the *butter* or *margarine* in a 12-inch skillet over medium heat. Add one *chop* and rub over bottom of pan so butter is spread evenly. Add remaining chops and cook until well browned and tender. Time depends on thickness of chops. Move and stack cooked chops to one side of skillet.

Place *green pepper* in empty space in skillet. Move skillet so peppers are over heat. Fry peppers until tender yet crisp.

Pour *tomato sauce* over peppers. Add *mushrooms, potatoes* and seasonings. Stir and mix together.

Arrange chops and vegetables so bottom of skillet is covered. Cook over medium low heat, stirring and turning occasionally until vegetables are hot.

MENU SUGGESTION

Serve with green leafy vegetable, celery sticks, whole wheat bread, fresh fruit or cookies, milk, and coffee or tea.

Stir-Fry Chicken With Vegetables

Makes 4 servings

2	teaspoons cornstarch
1/2	teaspoon salt
	Pepper to taste
2	tablespoons soy sauce
2	tablespoons water
2	tablespoons oil
1	onion, chopped
1	cup coarsely chopped celery
1	green pepper, thinly sliced
1	cup cooked green beans
1	can (4-ounce) mushrooms, well drained (Reserve liquid to use in this recipe.)
2	cups cooked chicken or turkey, cut into bite-size pieces
	Reserved mushroom liquid plus enough chicken broth to measure 3/4 cup liquid

Blend *cornstarch, salt, pepper, soy sauce* and *water* in a cup. Set aside.

Heat *oil* until hot over medium heat in a large fry pan with a tight-fitting cover.

Add *onion* and *celery.* Stir-fry for 3 minutes.

Add *green pepper, green beans* and well-drained *mushrooms.* Stir-fry all the vegetables for 2 minutes longer.

Stir in *chicken* or *turkey* and *mushroom–chicken broth* mixture. Bring to a boil. Cover. Reduce heat slightly and cook 3 minutes. Vegetables will be crisp.

Stir in cornstarch mixture. Cook over medium low heat, stirring to prevent sticking, until thickened. Serve at once.

•

Skillet All-in-One Ham Meal

Makes 4 servings

- 1/2 cup orange or pineapple juice
- 2 tablespoons honey
- 1/4 teaspoon cinnamon
- Dash cloves
- Dash nutmeg

- 4 tablespoons butter or margarine

- 4 servings sliced, boiled, canned or home-cooked ham

- 1 can (1 pound 2 ounces) vacuum-pack sweet potatoes or yams with liquid, sliced into 1/2-inch-thick pieces (When packed in large amount of liquid, be sure to drain well.)

- 1 can (1 pound) green beans, drained, or more if appetites call for them

Measure the *orange* or *pineapple juice* and *honey* into a measuring cup. Stir in *cinnamon, cloves* and *nutmeg*. If desired, add more or less of the spices to suit your taste. Set aside.

Melt 2 tablespoons of the *butter* in a 12-inch skillet with a tight-fitting cover.

Add sliced *ham* and cook over medium low heat until ham is lightly browned. Push to one side of skillet.

Arrange the sliced *sweet potatoes* or *yams* in the empty space in skillet. Place skillet on stove so potatoes are over heat. Pour juice mixture over sweet potatoes. Stir and turn so juice mixture and potatoes are well mixed. Cover. Cook over medium low heat until potatoes are very warm.

Push potatoes to opposite side from ham.

Add and melt remaining 2 tablespoons butter to empty space between ham and sweet potatoes. Place drained *beans* in space between potatoes and ham. Place skillet on stove so beans are over heat. Cover. Cook over low heat until beans and potatoes are hot.

MENU SUGGESTION

Serve with cucumber and celery sticks, corn bread, strawberries, milk, and coffee or tea.

●

Hash in a Hurry

Makes 4 servings

4	tablespoons butter or margarine
2/3	cup chopped onion
2	cups diced or ground, cooked roast beef, ham, pork, chicken or turkey
3	cups diced, cold cooked potatoes
1/2 to 1	teaspoon salt
	Pepper to taste
1/2	cup milk

Melt *butter* in a 12-inch skillet.

Add *onions* and cook over medium low heat until tender. Do not brown.

Gently stir in the *meat* and *potatoes. Salt* and *pepper* to taste.

Pour *milk* over meat-potato mixture. Cook 20 to 25 minutes or until crusty and brown. Stir and turn occasionally to prevent sticking.

VARIATION

• Chopped green pepper (1/4 to 1/2 cup) may be added and cooked with onion.

MENU SUGGESTION

Serve with brussels sprouts, tossed salad, rye bread, an orange and cookies, milk, and coffee or tea.

Sausage-and-Corn Main Dish

Makes 4 servings

3/4 pound smoked sausage (more if
desired), cut into 1- to 1 1/2-inch
pieces

1 medium onion, thinly sliced

1 can (1-pound) tomatoes

1 can (12-ounce size, vacuum pack) corn
(2 cans for families with big appetites)
Salt and pepper to taste

Place *sausage* in a large skillet. Cook over medium low
heat until some fat is given off.

Add *onion.* Cook until onion is tender and sausage
lightly browned. Spoon off and discard all but 1 tablespoon fat given off by sausage.

Add *tomatoes.* Mash or cut tomatoes when they are
whole. Bring mixture to a boil. Lower heat. Cover. Simmer (keep liquid below a boil but still moving) for 20
minutes.

Add *corn.* Cook only until corn is hot. Taste. Add seasonings if needed. Stir and serve.

MENU SUGGESTION

Serve with broccoli, cucumber sticks, crusty bread,
an apple or applesauce, milk, and coffee or tea.

Lima Bean Main Dish

Makes 4 servings

> 1 tablespoon butter or margarine
>
> 1 medium onion, chopped
>
> 1/2 cup water
> 1 can (8-ounce) tomato sauce or 1 cup tomato sauce
>
> 2 packages (10 ounces each) frozen lima beans or 1 bag (20-ounce) frozen lima beans
> 1 teaspoon salt
>
> 1 cup (1/4 pound) shredded Cheddar cheese

Melt *butter* or *margarine* in a large skillet with tight-fitting cover.

Add *onion.* Cook over low heat until just tender. Do not brown.

Stir in *water* and *tomato sauce.* Mix until well blended. Cook over medium heat until hot.

Stir in *lima beans* and *salt.* Cover. Simmer (keep liquid below a boil but still moving) until beans are tender, about 20 minutes. Add more water, if needed.

Spread *cheese* evenly over beans. Cover and heat until cheese is just melted. Serve at once. Do not overcook or cheese will be watery.

Note: Well-drained, cooked, fresh, dried or canned beans may be used in place of frozen beans.

MENU SUGGESTION

Serve with deviled eggs, big, green leafy and raw
vegetable salad, rye bread, fresh fruit and cookies, milk,
and coffee or tea.

Noodle-Cheese Skillet Main Dish

Makes 4 servings

> 4 tablespoons butter or margarine
>
> 1 onion, chopped
>
> 1/2 pound (8 ounces) noodles, cooked and
>   drained
>
> 1 1/2 cups cottage cheese, at room
>   temperature
>   Salt to taste

Melt *butter* or *margarine* in a large skillet.

Add *onion.* Cook over low heat until tender but not
browned.

Stir in cooked *noodles.* Cook over medium heat, stirring constantly, until noodles are a golden color.

Remove from heat. Gently stir in *salt* and *cottage
cheese.* Mix well and serve.

Egg Ideas

Eggs which are usually on hand lend themselves to last-minute meals at the end of a busy day. What could be easier than scrambled eggs for dinner? They can be served plain or dressed up with a small amount of the following foods which are stirred into the egg mixture along with an herb or blended herbs just before scrambling.

- Chopped cooked ham
- Crumbled cheese
- Chopped canned sardines
- Flaked tuna
- Cooked sausage pieces
- Fresh or canned mushrooms
- Cooked vegetables
- Herb or blended herbs to suit your taste
- Cooked shrimp or crab
- Cooked chicken livers
- Cottage cheese

When there is more time, don't overlook the omelet, egg and cheese soufflé, and hard-cooked egg in dishes such as creamed eggs and mushrooms, Creole eggs, and egg salad.

Basic Pan Sauce for Creamed Dishes

Makes about 2 cups

>   1/4   cup flour
>   3/4   teaspoon salt
>   Dash pepper
>
>   2   cups milk, or 1 cup milk plus 1 cup
>   chicken broth, or pan drippings of
>   roasts plus enough liquid such as milk
>   or meat broths to measure 2 cups

Measure the *flour, salt* and *pepper* into saucepan. Stir until well mixed.

Stir into flour mixture a few tablespoons of *liquid* at a time to make a smooth paste. Gradually add remaining liquid, stirring after each addition, to make a smooth mixture.

Cook over medium low heat, stirring constantly, until sauce starts to thicken. Reduce heat and cook over low heat, stirring constantly, until sauce has thickened.

VARIATIONS

- Savory Mustard Pan Sauce: Add 1/2 teaspoon paprika, few drops onion juice, and 1/2 to 1 teaspoon dry mustard with flour.
- Cheese Sauce: Add 1 cup shredded, sharp Cheddar cheese to basic pan sauce. Stir in just until cheese is melted.

• Curry Sauce: Mix 1 teaspoon curry powder and 1/4 teaspoon ginger root with flour. For more highly seasoned sauce, add cayenne.

FLAVOR TIPS

Make your own zesty, flavorful sauces by adding herbs or spices or a blend of herbs and spices, or boosters such as cooked mushrooms, celery, onion, pimiento, etc., or pan drippings as part of the liquid in basic pan sauce.

Creamed Main Dishes

CREAMED HAM AND MIXED VEGETABLES

Add 2 cups chopped cooked ham and 1 1/2 cups cooked mixed vegetables to 2 cups Basic Pan Sauce for Creamed Dishes above. Heat until ham and mixed vegetables are hot. Serve with rice or noodles.

CREAMED CHICKEN AND CORN

Add 2 cups chopped cooked chicken and 1 1/2 cups cooked corn to 2 cups Savory Mustard Pan Sauce above. Heat until chicken and corn are hot. Serve over cooked broccoli.

CREAMED TUNA AND PEAS

Add 1 can (6 1/2 to 7 ounces) tuna and 2 cups peas to 2 cups Curry Pan Sauce above. Heat until hot. Serve over rice, noodles or toasted bread.

Baked Bean Quickies

HAMBURGER SKILLET MEAL

Cook hamburger until almost done. Add canned baked beans, seasonings to taste, and cooked (canned, fresh or frozen) green beans. Cook over low heat until beans are hot. Serve with tossed salad, dark bread, an orange, milk, and coffee or tea.

HAM AND BEAN SANDWICH MEAL

Place sliced bread on plate. Top with sliced boiled or home-cooked ham. Top with hot baked beans (canned) seasoned to your taste. Sprinkle with grated cheese. Serve with large portion of carrot-cabbage slaw, fresh fruit, milk, and coffee or tea.

CHEESE AND BEAN SANDWICH MEAL

Place sliced bread on plate. Top with thinly sliced cheese. Top with hot baked beans. Serve with cooked cabbage, finger salad of raw carrot chunks and green pepper rings, fruit, milk, and coffee or tea.

Pizza PDQ

Makes 4 servings

    1   loaf (14 to 16 inches long) Italian or Vienna bread, cut in half lengthwise

    1   cup tomato sauce
1/4   cup water
    1   tablespoon oil
    1   teaspoon oregano
       Salt to taste

1/4   pound thinly sliced salami or peperoni or 3/4 cup well-seasoned, cooked ground beef or crumbled, cooked meat loaf
1/2   pound mozzarella cheese, shredded or thinly sliced

       Parmesan cheese
       Additional oregano and salt to sprinkle on pizza

Split *bread* in half lengthwise. Place on baking sheet or aluminum foil, split side up. Set aside.

Pour *tomato sauce* into a small saucepan. Add *water, oil, oregano,* and *salt.* Stir and mix well. Heat until hot. Spread half the sauce over the bread halves.

Arrange *salami* and *cheese* over bread halves. Spoon remaining sauce evenly over top of pizza.

Sprinkle lightly with *Parmesan cheese* and additional salt and oregano, if desired.

Place in preheated 400° F. oven and bake until cheese is soft and bubbly and bread is hot, about 15 to 20 minutes. Or pizza may be cooked by placing under broiler until cheese is soft and bubbly and bread is hot.

NOTE

- When Italian bread is not available, use split English muffins, hard rolls, or sliced bread.
- Toppings for pizza may also include cooked green pepper, mushrooms, cooked sausage, anchovies, etc.

Hot Tuna Burger

Makes 4 servings

1	can (6 1/2 to 7 ounces) tuna, drained and flaked
1/2 to 2/3	cup tomato catsup
1/2	cup (2 ounces) cut-up or shredded cheese
1/2 to 2/3	cup chopped celery or bean sprouts
4	buns, split

Place the *tuna, tomato catsup, cheese* and *celery* or *bean sprouts* in a bowl. Mix well.

Fill split *buns* with tuna mixture. Wrap each burger in aluminum foil. Bake in 375° F. oven for 15 minutes or until heated through.

MENU SUGGESTION

Serve with split pea soup, finger salad, peaches, milk, and coffee or tea.

Vegetable Tips

MIX AND MATCH

Instead of cooking each vegetable in separate pots, take your cue from the frozen food industry, and cook two or more in the same pot. For example, combine broccoli and cauliflower, or cook carrots and potatoes together, or carrots, potatoes, and green beans.

STEW

Don't overlook a quick vegetable stew of tomatoes, zucchini, sliced potato, with green pepper and onion for flavoring.

STEAM

When cooking two vegetables in the same pot, use a food steamer which allows for cooking two or more vegetables while retaining the distinctive flavor of each.

The use of a pressure cooker can dramatically cut cooking time.

Easy-Do Prunes and Apricots

Makes 6 to 8 servings

> 2 cups water
> 1 cup prunes
> 1 cup dried apricots
>
> 2 cups prune juice
> Lemon juice to taste
> Cinnamon to taste

Pour *water* into a saucepan. Add *prunes* and *apricots*. Bring to a boil. Cover. Reduce heat and simmer 10 minutes.

Add *prune juice*. Stir in *lemon juice* and *cinnamon*.

Cool slightly. Place in container. Cover. Refrigerate overnight. For plumper fruit, refrigerate for 24 hours.

Easy-Do Applesauce Desserts

• Crumble nutbread or fruit bread into a dessert dish. Spoon applesauce over crumbled bread. Top with more crumbled nut or fruit bread.

• Spoon vanilla ice cream into a dessert dish. Spoon heated applesauce flavored with nutmeg and lemon juice over ice cream.

• Spoon sliced peaches into a dessert dish. Sprinkle granola over peaches. Cover with applesauce and additional granola.

• Spoon applesauce flavored with lemon and nutmeg over a square of gingerbread or spice cake.

Easy-Do Yogurt Desserts

• Spoon plain or vanilla yogurt over sliced strawberries. Sprinkle with chopped nuts.

• Toast raisin bread. Cut into small cubes and fold into plain or vanilla yogurt flavored with cinnamon and honey.

• Layer in a tall glass, yogurt, sliced peaches, yogurt, granola, sliced banana, yogurt and berries.

• Cut up a variety of fresh fruit and fold in yogurt which has been mixed with berries and honey.

• Spoon into plain or vanilla-flavored yogurt, honey, cinnamon and cookie crumbs.

7

Accordion Recipes

Accordion recipes are designed for easier cooking by working parents on working nights.

They look long but are not long in terms of work. These recipes take more space because they give tips and techniques for faster, more efficient cooking. They are clear and explicit. And remember, Accordion Recipes are actually three recipes in one. A bonus factor is that you can use the easy sauces in some of these recipes with second servings of leftover cooked meats you have on hand.

A final reminder: There will be no "leftover" taste in any of these dishes if you follow the recipes carefully, using the recommended low heat and only enough time to just heat the meat through rather than recook it.

The quantities of meat given will suit the average family but you may increase or decrease amounts according to your needs.

As in the case of the Quick and Easy recipes, the seasoning has been kept at a minimum level. Increase it, if you like, or change the seasoning to suit your taste.

The menu suggestions, as mentioned, are designed to give a nutritionally balanced meal. It's OK to make substitutions but check the charts at the end of the book to be sure you are choosing a food equivalent in nutrition to the one in the menu.

Accordion Recipes offer an option for solving the working parent's cooking problems. We hope that it will work for you.

GROUND BEEF ACCORDION RECIPE

Makes 4 to 6 meat patties, 8 slices meat loaf, and 4 servings of meatballs.

Cook meat for three ground-beef meals at one time. Then you will have cooked ground beef for three varied meals as follows: Meat Patties, Meat Loaf, and Meatballs for Spaghetti.

With the Meat Patties meal, first serve coleslaw with cheese bread to hold appetites until dinner is ready, then serve meat patties with relishes, parslied potatoes, green leafy vegetable, pears or other fresh fruit, milk, and coffee or tea.

Foods needed:

3/4	*cup tomato sauce or juice*
3	*medium-size eggs*
1	*medium-size onion, finely chopped*
2	*teaspoons salt*
1/2	*teaspoon black pepper, if desired*
5	*slices fresh whole wheat or white bread*
3	*pounds ground beef*

Measure into a large mixing bowl:

3/4	cup tomato sauce or juice
3	medium-size eggs
1	medium onion, finely chopped
2	teaspoons salt
1/2	teaspoon black pepper, if desired

Beat with a large mixing spoon until well blended.

Pull apart with fingers and crumble into very small pieces over tomato-egg mixture:

> 5 slices fresh whole wheat or white bread

Mix with large mixing spoon until all the bread is well moistened.

Add:

> 3 pounds ground beef

Mix until all the ingredients are thoroughly blended. Large amounts of ground meat are mixed most quickly and thoroughly using the hands (well washed). If mixture seems dry, add small amount of juice or sauce; if too wet, add small amount of crumbled bread. Texture varies because of differences in egg size, meat fat content, and degree of dryness in bread. If added bread or liquid is used, mix again thoroughly.

Divide mixture in half. Shape half the mixture into 2 small meat loaves for faster cooking. Place loaves at one end of large, shallow roasting pan, or large broiler pan.

Divide remaining half of meat mixture in half. Shape one-half into 4 to 6 patties. Arrange in single layer in pan with meat loaves. Shape remaining mixture into meatballs and reserve on waxed paper to save dishwashing.

Bake meat loaves and patties in preheated 350° F. oven for 15 to 20 minutes or until patties are done. Patties are cooked before they brown.

Remove meat patties to be used for dinner, and immediately arrange meatballs in roasting pan space where patties were cooked. Return to oven. Bake meat loaves and meatballs 20 to 25 minutes longer while the family is eating the meat pattie meal. When meat loaves and meatballs are done, remove from oven. Refrigerate as soon as possible.

Pan Sauce

Add to fat, pan drippings and browned bits in pan:

    1/2   cup water

Scrape pan with edge of pancake turner. Pour fat, drippings and bits into container. Cover. Refrigerate. Use to make pan sauce or gravy for meat-loaf meal.

●

Spaghetti and Meatballs Dinner

Makes 4 servings

First serve big green salad and crunchy bread to hold appetites. Then serve Spaghetti and Meatballs with cheese, broccoli, fresh or canned peaches, milk, and coffee or tea.

Foods needed:

2 to 3	*cups tomato sauce*
	Cooked meatballs
	Seasonings
1/2 to 2/3	*pound uncooked spaghetti, depending on family appetites*
	Salt
	Grated Parmesan cheese

Measure into a saucepan:

2 to 3   cups tomato sauce

Add:

Cooked meatballs
Seasonings to taste

Bring to a boil. Cover. Lower heat and simmer gently (keep liquid below a boil but still moving) while water comes to a boil for cooking spaghetti and while spaghetti cooks. Time is needed to blend the flavor of the sauce, meat and seasonings.

Cook according to package directions in boiling, salted water:

1/2 to 2/3   pound uncooked spaghetti

Drain spaghetti well.

Portion, and place on platter or in bowls. Spoon hot sauce and meatballs over spaghetti. Top with sprinkle of Parmesan cheese, if desired.

●

Meat Loaf Dinner

Makes 8 slices

With meat loaf dinner, first serve tomato juice and toast with cheese spread to hold appetites until dinner is ready. Then serve meat loaf with pan gravy and mashed potatoes, carrots, ice cream, milk, and coffee or tea.

Foods needed:

> *Reserved pan drippings from first*
> *cooking, with congealed fat removed*
> *Seasonings to taste*
> *Baked meat loaf, cut into 8 slices*

After removing congealed fat layer from pan drippings, pour into a 12-inch skillet:

Pan drippings

Cook over low heat until warmed through. Do not boil. Taste. Add seasonings of your choice. Cover and heat until hot.

Add:

Meat loaf slices

Cover. Simmer gently (keep drippings below a boil but still moving) until meat loaf is hot enough to serve. Important: Do not boil. This is what develops "left-over" taste.

VARIATIONS

- Mushrooms may be added to pan drippings.
- Pan drippings may be combined with tomato sauce before adding meat loaf.

ROAST CHICKEN ACCORDION RECIPE

Makes 12 ready-cooked servings

Chicken for three meals can be cooked at one time. Then you will have three varied chicken dishes as follows: Roast Chicken, Lemon Ginger Chicken, and Chicken Paprika.

With the Roast Chicken serve sweet potatoes, cauliflower, jellied cranberry sauce on chicory, dinner rolls, fresh or frozen melon balls, milk, and coffee or tea.

Foods needed:

> 3   *2 1/2 to 3 pound broiler/fryers, split in halves*

Preheat oven to 300° F.

Place in a very large, shallow roasting pan, large broiler pan, or roasting pans split side down so halves do not overlap:

> 3   2 1/2 to 3 pound broiler/fryers, split in halves

Place in oven. Bake for 2 hours, or until golden brown and done. For juicier chicken, do not turn. May be basted with pan drippings, if desired. However, chicken browns without basting. Remove chicken from oven. Serve 1 chicken for dinner.

Refrigerate remaining chicken immediately after dinner and before cleanup.

PAN SAUCE

After removing chicken from roasting pan, pour 3/4 cup water in pan. Stir and scrape to loosen browned bits. Pour water-fat mixture into container. Cover. Refrigerate. Remove congealed fat when ready to use and use drippings for pan sauce or gravy.

•

Lemon Ginger Chicken Dinner

Makes 4 servings

Serve with rice, broccoli, tossed salad, bread, applesauce or fresh apples, milk, and coffee or tea.

Foods needed:

2	*teaspoons cornstarch*
1	*tablespoon water*
1/2	*cup water*
1/4	*cup soy sauce*
1/4	*teaspoon ground ginger, or to taste*
2	*tablespoons lemon juice*
1/4	*cup finely chopped onion, if desired*
2	*tablespoons oil*
1	*ready-roasted chicken, cut into serving pieces*

Measure into a cup and blend until well mixed:

2	teaspoons cornstarch
1	tablespoon water

Set aside.

Combine and mix well in a measuring cup:

1/2	cup water
1/4	cup soy sauce
1/4	teaspoon ground ginger, or to taste
2	tablespoons lemon juice
1/4	cup finely chopped onion

Set aside.

Measure into a 12-inch skillet with tight-fitting cover:

>   2   tablespoons oil

Heat over medium low heat until hot.

Add:

>   1   roasted chicken, cut into serving-size
>   pieces (chicken heats faster when you
>   separate leg from thigh, wing from
>   breast, and cut breast in half)

Heat on each side for 3 to 4 minutes.

Carefully pour over chicken:

>   Ginger-lemon-soy mixture

Cover and heat over low heat until chicken is hot. Turn pieces occasionally. When chicken is hot, move pieces to one side of skillet, and stack pieces on top of one another.

Stir into empty space over hot soy mixture:

>   Cornstarch-water mixture

Tilt skillet back and forth so liquid in pan is mixed with cornstarch. Cook, while stirring, until pan sauce is thickened.

Arrange chicken to cover bottom of pan and spoon sauce over chicken. Heat for an additional minute.

Serve chicken. Spoon sauce over chicken.

Note: Taste before adding salt since degree of saltiness in soy sauce varies from brand to brand.

Chicken Paprika

Makes 4 servings

Serve Chicken Paprika with buttered noodles, spinach, sliced tomatoes, rye bread, blueberries or other fresh fruit, milk, and coffee or tea.

Foods needed:

2	*tablespoons oil*
1/2	*cup chopped onion*
1/4	*teaspoon black pepper*
1	*roasted chicken, cut into serving-size pieces*
1	*teaspoon salt, or to taste*
2/3	*cup water*
1	*teaspoon paprika, or to taste*
1	*cup sour cream, or more, depending on amount of sauce desired*

Measure into a 12-inch skillet with tight-fitting cover:

2   tablespoons oil

Heat over medium low heat until hot.

Add:

1/2   cup chopped onion
1/4   teaspoon black pepper

Cook until onion is soft and tender but not browned.

Add:

      1   roasting chicken, cut into serving-size
            pieces
      1   teaspoon salt
   2/3   cup water

Bring just to the boiling point. Reduce heat to low. Cover and heat only until chicken is hot. Place chicken in serving dish or bowl and keep hot.

Stir into pan sauce in skillet:

      1   teaspoon paprika or to taste

Stir and mix until paprika is dissolved.

Stir in:

      1   cup sour cream

Stir and mix well, over low heat, until sour cream mixture is hot. Do not boil. Spoon over hot chicken and serve.

ROAST BEEF ACCORDION RECIPE

Makes 12 servings ready-cooked beef

Cook a 3 1/2-pound beef rump roast. You'll have meat for a roast beef dinner as well as ready-cooked meat for Barbecued Beef Slices and Beef Dip Sandwiches in the time it takes to cook one roast.

Serve the roast beef with steamed potatoes and pan gravy, mixed vegetables, spinach salad, rolls, ice cream and cookies, milk, and coffee or tea.

Foods needed:

*3 1/2 to 4   pound beef rump roast, or amount
                needed for 3 meals for your family*

Place on rack in open roasting pan:

Rump roast

Insert meat thermometer so it is centered in the thickest part of meat. Tip should not rest in fat.

Roast in preheated 350° F. oven until meat thermometer reaches degree of doneness desired, 140° F. for rare, 160° F. for medium, 170° F. for well-done. Time varies with thickness and shape of roast.

Remove roast from oven. Place on platter or cutting surface. Allow to stand or "rest" for 15 to 20 minutes for easier slicing.

While meat rests, make a pan sauce or gravy from pan drippings.

After 15 to 20 minutes, slice 4 servings of roast beef for dinner. Leave remainder of meat to cool during dinner. Pack and refrigerate as soon as possible.

●

Barbecued Beef Slices

Makes 4 servings

Serve Barbecued Beef Slices over steamed rice with green leafy vegetable, finger foods such as cucumber sticks and celery stalks, crusty bread, orange and cookies, milk, and coffee or tea.

Foods needed:

2	*tablespoons butter or margarine*
2	*medium onions, thinly sliced*
4	*servings thinly sliced, ready-cooked roast beef*
3/4	*cup catsup*
3/4	*cup water*
1	*tablespoon vinegar or lemon juice*
1 to 2	*teaspoons chili powder*
	Salt to taste

Melt in a 12-inch skillet with tight-fitting cover:

2   tablespoons butter or margarine

Add:

2   medium onions, thinly sliced

Cook over medium low heat, stirring occasionally, until tender yet crisp. Do not brown. When tender, push to one side of skillet.

Place in skillet:

4   servings thinly sliced ready-cooked roast beef

Move skillet so beef slices are over heat. Cook over low heat just long enough to heat through. Turn once or twice to shorten heating time. Push to one side.

Add to empty area in skillet:

3/4	cup catsup
3/4	cup water
1	tablespoon vinegar or lemon juice
1 to 2	teaspoons chili powder
	Salt to taste

Cook over medium low heat until hot, stirring occasionally to mix and prevent sticking.

Mix sauce with beef and onions. Cover. Cook over low heat, stirring occasionally, for about 10 minutes, or until onions are cooked. Serve.

●

Beef Dip Sandwich

Makes 4 servings

Serve Beef Dip Sandwich with a big serving of carrot and cabbage slaw, fresh fruit, milk, and coffee or tea.

Foods needed:

> 2 1/4   *cups beef or chicken broth*
> 1   *can (4-ounce) mushrooms, pieces and stems, including liquid*
> *Bottled hot pepper sauce or other seasonings to taste*
> 4   *servings thinly sliced ready-cooked roast beef*
> *Hard rolls or crusty French or Italian bread, enough for 4 sandwiches*

Pour into medium-size skillet:

> 2 1/4   cups beef or chicken broth
> 1   can mushrooms, pieces and stems, and liquid
> Bottled hot pepper sauce or other seasonings to taste

Cook over medium low heat until hot.

Add:

> 4   servings thinly sliced cooked roast beef

Cook over low heat until beef is hot.

Pour into 4 small bowls or tea cups an equal amount of broth, reserving ¾ cup of broth, meat and mushrooms in skillet.

Place on each dinner plate:

> Roll, cut in half, or bread cut lengthwise into sandwich portions

Spoon on half a roll on each plate 2 to 3 tablespoons reserved broth. Spoon equal amounts of mushrooms over broth-moistened roll half. Add meat over mushrooms. Top with other half of roll.

Dip sandwich in broth and eat away, each helping himself to broth in individual bowls or tea cups.

VARIATION

Use onion soup in place of broth and mushrooms.

•

PORK ROAST ACCORDION RECIPE

Makes 12 servings ready-cooked pork

Cook a 3 1/2-pound rolled pork roast. You'll have ready-cooked pork for a roast pork dinner as well as Glazed Pork and Pork Fried Rice for two other meals. And all this meat in the time it takes to cook the roast.

Round out the first meal of Roast Pork with pan gravy, lemon broccoli, oven-browned potatoes, sliced tomatoes, whole wheat bread, fresh fruit, milk, and coffee or tea.

Foods needed:

3 1/2 to 4   pound rolled pork loin roast

Place on rack in open roasting pan:

3 1/2 to 4   pound rolled pork roast

Insert meat thermometer so it is centered in the thickest part of meat. Tip should not rest in fat. Roast in preheated 325° F. oven. Roast until meat thermometer reaches 170° F. Remove roast from oven. Place on platter or cutting surface. Allow to stand or "rest" for 15 minutes for easier slicing.

While meat rests, make a pan sauce or gravy from pan drippings.

After 15 minutes, slice 4 servings roast pork for dinner. Leave remainder of meat to cool during dinner. Pack and refrigerate as soon as dinner is over.

●

Glazed Pork Dinner

Makes 4 servings

Make Glazed Pork and serve with buttered noodles, green beans, finger salad, bread, an orange, cookies, milk, and coffee or tea.

Foods needed:

> 1/2   *cup chili sauce*
> 1   *tablespoon vinegar*
> 2   *tablespoons oil, butter or margarine*
> 2   *medium-size green peppers, cut into thin slices*
> 2   *medium onions, cut into thin slices, if desired*
> 4   *servings thinly sliced, ready-cooked pork*

Measure into cup:

> 1/2   cup chili sauce
> 1   tablespoon vinegar

Mix well and set aside.

Melt in a 12-inch skillet:

> 2   tablespoons oil, butter or margarine

Add:

> 2   medium-size green peppers, cut into slices
> 2   medium-size onions, thinly sliced

Cook, stirring occasionally, over medium low heat. Do not brown. Cook only until fork tender and crunchy. Push pepper and onions to one side of skillet.

Arrange in pan:

> 4 servings thinly sliced, ready-cooked pork

Center meat in skillet over heat. Using low heat, cook slices on each side about 2 minutes.

Spoon over meat:

> Chili sauce–vinegar mixture

Gently stir and mix with green peppers and onions. Cover. Heat only until hot. Remember, meat is already cooked.

•

Pork Fried Rice

Makes 4 servings

Serve with Swiss chard or other green leafy vegetable, finger salad, whole wheat bread, pineapple chunks, milk, and coffee or tea.

Foods needed:

2	*tablespoons oil or other fat*
2	*eggs*
1/3	*cup finely chopped onion*
1/2	*cup finely chopped celery stalk and leaves*
1 1/2	*cups slivered ready-cooked pork*
3	*cups cooked rice (4 cups for big eaters)*
2 to 3	*tablespoons soy sauce*
	Salt, only if needed

Heat in a 12-inch skillet:

> 2   tablespoons oil

Add, and fry over low heat:

> 2   eggs

Turn and cook until yolk is firm. Remove skillet from heat. Using edge of turner, cut eggs in skillet into shreds. Push egg to side of pan. Return to heat.

Add:

> 1/3   cup finely chopped onion
> 1/2   cup finely chopped celery

Cook, stirring occasionally, until onion is tender. Do not brown. Move onion and celery to side of pan with cooked egg.

Add:

    1 1/2   cups slivered ready-cooked pork

Heat for 2 to 3 minutes. Stir and mix into vegetable and egg mixture.

Spoon over meat mixture:

    3   cups cooked rice

Sprinkle with:

    2 to 3   tablespoons soy sauce
            Salt, only if needed

Cook over medium low heat, stirring gently, until rice is hot. Serve immediately.

●

SAUSAGE ACCORDION RECIPE

Makes 12 servings of ready-cooked sausage

Cook enough sausage for three meals at one time, and you'll have meat for a sausage dinner, a sausage and sweet potato dinner, and a hot hero sandwich dinner.

Serve first sausage dinner with tomato juice and crackers to hold appetites until dinner is ready, then sausage, buttered mashed potatoes, carrots, fresh fruit of your choice, cookies, milk, and coffee or tea.

Foods needed:

> 3   *pounds Italian-style sausage, separated into links, or cut into 4-inch pieces*

Place in a large, shallow baking pan in a single layer:

> 3   pounds cut-up sausage

Bake in a preheated 300° F. oven for about 45 minutes to 1 hour, or until done. Thickness of sausage and length of links determines cooking time. Turn and baste with pan juices from sausage two or three times during roasting. Remove from oven.

Serve one-third of cooked sausage as meat course for first meal.

Allow remaining sausage to cool while eating. Pack and refrigerate as soon as possible.

PAN SAUCE

Add to sausage fat, drippings and browned bits in roasting pan:

1/2   cup water

Scrape with edge of pancake turner to loosen browned bits. Pour fat, drippings and bits into container; cover and refrigerate for future use. Fat that rises to the top while refrigerated may be used in following recipe and the remaining drippings used for Pan Sauce for another meal.

●

Sausage and Sweet Potato Skillet Meal

Makes 4 servings

With this meal, first serve a finger salad of cucumber spears, watercress, tomato wedges and cheese strips to hold appetites until dinner, then serve sausage and sweet potatoes with cauliflower, bread, fresh fruit of your choice, cookies, milk, and coffee or tea.

Foods needed:

2	*tablespoons butter, margarine or sausage fat*
4	*servings ready-cooked sausage, cut into bite-size pieces*
4 to 6	*medium-size cooked (fresh or canned) sweet potatoes or yams, cut into 1/2-inch-thick pieces*
1/2	*cup orange or pineapple juice*
1/4	*teaspoon cinnamon*
	Dash nutmeg
	Dash cloves
2	*tablespoons honey*

Melt in a 12-inch skillet over low heat:

2	tablespoons butter, margarine or sausage fat

Arrange in skillet:

4	servings cut-up cooked sausage
4 to 6	medium-size cooked sweet potatoes, cut into 1/2-inch-thick pieces

Cook over medium low heat.

Meanwhile, measure into a cup and mix well:

1/2	cup orange or pineapple juice
1/4	teaspoon cinnamon
	Dash nutmeg
	Dash cloves
2	tablespoons honey

Pour orange juice–spice mixture over sausage and sweet potatoes. Stir gently and mix with sausage and sweet potatoes. Cover. Lower heat and cook until sausage and potatoes are hot. Serve.

•

Italian Sausage and Green Pepper Hero Meal

Makes 4 servings

Serve Hero with extra-large mixed green salad, sherbet, milk, and coffee or tea.

Foods needed:

> 2 *tablespoons butter, margarine or*
> *sausage fat*
> 2 *medium-size green peppers, cut into*
> *thin slices to cook faster*
> 2 *medium-size onions, cut into thin slices*
> *to cook faster*
> 4 *servings ready-cooked sausage, cut into*
> *bite-size pieces*
> 1 *cup tomato sauce*
> *Salt and pepper to taste*
> *Oregano, or blend of herbs, to taste*
> 4 *hard rolls or 4 crunchy bread wedges,*
> *split*

Melt and heat in a 12-inch skillet with tight-fitting cover:

> 2 tablespoons butter, margarine or
> sausage fat

Add:

> 2 medium-size peppers, thinly sliced
> 2 medium-size onions, thinly sliced

Cover over medium low heat until onions and peppers are tender yet crisp. Do not brown.

Add and stir in:

> 4   servings ready-cooked sausage, cut
>   into bite-size pieces
> 1   cup tomato sauce
>   Salt and pepper to taste
>   Oregano, or blend of herbs, to taste

Cover. Cook over low heat just long enough for the sausage and tomato sauce to get hot. Stir occasionally to prevent sticking. Remember, sausage is already cooked. Taste. If necessary, adjust seasonings. Cover. Simmer 2 minutes longer.

Spoon into split hard rolls or crunchy bread wedges. Serve.

●

8

Throw Together Meals

When you're tired out, when the kids have all come home with disappointing report cards and adult tempers are torn to shreds, that's the time to resort to a Throw Together Meal. People can't always cook like clockwork. There's a human factor. For those who can't stand cooking, TTMs are a lifesaver. It's a change from eating out every night or a perpetual parade of "take-ins."

These Throw Together Meals have two things that

most TTMs don't have. They are planned for contrasts in flavor, texture and appearance to make a nice meal; and the combinations of food are nutritionally balanced. It must be admitted that many throw together meals pay little attention to nutrition. They are often skimpy and leave you lacking in the well-filled feeling which follows a good meal.

Most of these meals involve little more than putting bought, ready-prepared foods on the table. Each member of the family puts the foods together to make a cold plate, sandwich or salad to suit himself. This keeps the cook out of the kitchen and offers a pleasing choice. Working parents tell us that children sometimes fuss about eating all the foods put before them. TTMs offer a holiday for kids to choose what they like and eat the way they like. Of course, no parent needs to be told that children should not be encouraged to leave out of a meal foods that they need for good health.

Besides the suggestions that follow, it's a good idea to keep certain foods on hand for those emergency "can't stand cooking" nights. Keep a stock of nutritious protein foods such as canned fish, cottage cheese, and other cheeses. Eggs are a fine protein food to keep on hand, especially when they are hard-cooked in advance, ready for instant eating in a cold plate, salad, or sandwich.

Hurry-Scurry Platter Meal

Arrange attractively on one big platter or tray:

Ham Slices
Cheese Slices

Help yourself finger foods:

Cherry Tomatoes
Watercress Sprigs

Three Bean Salad
Dark Pumpernickel Bread
Chow Chow Relish or Mustard

Apricots, canned or fresh
Oatmeal Cookies

Milk
Coffee or Tea

For hearty eaters, add soup or juice.

THREE BEAN SALAD

Empty into a bowl well-drained canned green beans, yellow wax beans, and fully-cooked canned kidney beans. Sprinkle with basil or other herb or herbs of your choice. Add zesty Italian or French dressing. Toss lightly. *Note:* Add chopped onion or fresh green onion tops, if desired.

Throw Together Knife and Fork Sandwich Meal

Make your own layered sandwiches at table to eat with knife and fork:

Whole Wheat Bread
Mustard
Muenster Cheese Slices
Coleslaw, ready-made or Do Ahead
Roast Beef Slices

Help yourself finger foods:

Carrot Chunks
Celery Stalks
Orange Quarters

Easy-Do Yogurt Dessert

Milk
Coffee or Tea

For hearty eaters, add soup or juice.

EASY-DO YOGURT DESSERT

Alternate layers of granola, plain or vanilla yogurt, and sliced banana, with granola as top layer. Arrange in bowls, parfait or tall glasses.

Quick Chick Throw Together Meal

Use your own Do Ahead or ready-made:

Rotisserie Chicken
Potato Salad

Make your own salad at table:

Spinach Leaves
Raw Bean Sprouts, rinsed
Tomatoes
Dressing

Oatmeal Bread

Make your own Easy-Do Applesauce Dessert at table.

Milk
Coffee or Tea

For hearty eaters, add soup or juice.

EASY-DO APPLESAUCE DESSERT

Crumble cookies into a dessert dish. Spoon applesauce over cookie crumbs. Sprinkle with cinnamon or nutmeg. Top with sliced strawberries, blueberries, or sliced peaches.

Fish Throw Together Meal

Make your own salad at table:

Sardines
Tuna
Cottage Cheese
Mayonnaise
Asparagus pieces, canned
Radishes
Cucumber, washed and sliced
Tomatoes
Dark greens, such as Escarole,
Chicory and Watercress
Dressing

Pumpernickel Bread

Eat out of hand foods for dessert:

Dried Apricots, Prunes, or Raisins
Nuts
Oatmeal Cookies

Milk
Coffee or Tea

For hearty eaters, add soup or juice.

Table Salad Throw Together Meal

Make your own salad at table:

Cold Cooked Shrimp,
fresh from fish market,
canned or frozen
Hard-Cooked Eggs, Do Ahead
Cherry Tomatoes
Green Beans, canned
Watercress or Spinach Leaves
Fully Cooked Chick Peas or
Kidney Beans, canned
Thousand Island Dressing

Bran Muffins

Yogurt or Ice Cream with
Frozen Raspberries
or Other Fruit

Milk
Coffee or Tea

For hearty eaters, add soup or juice.

Let's Celebrate Throw Together Meal

When you're too tired to cook but the family has a reason to really celebrate, make your own platter:

Cooked Lobster or Crab Meat,
fresh from fish store, canned or frozen
Avocado
Watercress Sprigs
Cherry Tomatoes
Asparagus Spears, canned
Dressing, thick, to your liking

Croissants, or Crusty Bread Chunks

Brie or Other Soft Cheese
Crackers
Fresh Fruit

Milk
Coffee or Tea

Bird 'n' Beef Throw Together Meal

Make your own sandwiches at table:

Turkey
Corned Beef or Pastrami
Rye Bread
Mustard, Mayonnaise, etc.

Combo Easy-Do Salad

Help yourself finger foods:

Spinach Leaves
Raw Asparagus or
Zucchini Spears in season
Celery Stalks

Grapefruit Sections, canned
Cookies

Milk
Coffee or Tea

For hearty eaters, add soup or juice.

COMBO EASY-DO SALAD

Combine and mix canned, well-drained green beans, chick peas, and pickled beets with an herb and salad dressing of your choice. Add onion if you like.

Friday Throw Together Meal

This Throw Together Meal uses all those good leftovers lurking in the refrigerator that aren't enough to make a full meal but together add up to good food, a clear-the-refrigerator meal.

Cottage Cheese
Cheese Slices or Pieces
Cold Meat Slices
Hard-Cooked Eggs
Peanut Butter
Leftover Crunchies, such as Dark Green Leafy Salad
Greens, Raw Cauliflowerets, etc.

Pieces of Good Bread

Fresh Fruit in a Bowl

Milk
Coffee or Tea

For hearty eaters, add soup or juice.

Throw Together Meal, Boston Style

Each make your own hot sandwich at table:

> Hard Roll, split
> Ham Slices
> Cheese Slices

Top with:

> Hot Baked Beans, canned
> Coleslaw, bought or Do Ahead

Help yourself finger salad:

> Celery Stalks
> Carrot Chunks
> Green Pepper Rings

> Fresh Melon or Frozen Melon Balls
> Cookies

> Milk
> Coffee or Tea

9

Cooking Is Easier, Faster, If Pots Are Right

Just as the layout of the kitchen can make cooking easier, so can the kind of cookware used. Pots can make or break efficient cooking, especially those used on top of the stove. It is important for fast, thorough cooking of some dishes that pots have tight-fitting lids. Then steam will be created inside the pot for more rapid cooking. When the pot is used uncovered, or with a loosely-fitting lid, the steam escapes. The cooking is slower, and the food is not as succulent or tender.

High heat is often to blame for cooking failures. It results in poorly cooked, dried out, or burned food. When recipes call for low heat, medium heat, or simmering, it is essential to follow these directions carefully. A pot made with too thin a layer, or gauge, of metal, used over high heat, also leads to many cooking failures. The gauge of the metal in pots is crucial to cooking success. The metal should be thick enough to give an even distribution and retention of heat.

There are other efficiency factors to consider which are covered in Basic Utensils for Efficient Cooking, below, and in the following guidelines for purchasing pots and pans that make for easier, more rapid cooking. Once you decide which utensil is best for you, it is all-important to follow the manufacturer's instructions carefully for use and care.

Cookware Buying Guidelines

• A pot or pan to be used on top of the stove should be made of material that is a good heat conductor. This is most readily available in aluminum utensils of medium to heavy gauge (thickness).

• Sides of pots should be straight to conserve heat.

• A pot with a flat base makes the best contact with heat. Choose this type of pot or a flat-bottomed pot with a concave base which is designed to flatten on heating.

• A tight-fitting cover on a pot is essential to hold the steam within the pan. This reduces cooking time and conserves flavor. "Tight-fitting" does not mean a lid jammed on a pot. It means that it is close or snug fitting so that there is a minimum loss of moisture. This is especially important for working parents who usually have to cook as rapidly and efficiently as possible.

• Handles should be of proper weight and balance so that a pan does not tilt and tip over.

• Consider utensils that suit the design of your stove top, and take into account the amount of food to be cooked. If your range, for example, has a controlled-heat burner, a double boiler may not be needed for making delicate foods such as sauces, custards, etc.

• Buy utensils whose construction and finish make it easiest for you to care for them. There should be no seams, ridges, crevices or rough edges on the inside of the pot. These make the pot hard to clean and tend to accumulate food and bacteria.

• Before you buy, ask to see the manufacturer's pamphlets covering construction, use and care of the cookware. If you study these carefully, you may avoid spending money for a utensil that does not fit your needs as a working parent. For example, if several members of the family use the cookware, and some have a tendency to use high heat, you may decide not to buy cookware that will develop heat spots. This factor may be detected if the manufacturer's directions specify using the cookware over medium or low heat. To use this pot successfully, the manufacturer's instructions must be followed explicitly. The use and care leaflet for pots with copper bottoms may also give you a cue. Although these utensils do a good job of cooking, the leaflet stresses correctly that the pots should be cleaned with a good copper cleaner. To shine copper means extra maintenance work. In the instructions accompanying one manufacturer's aluminum pots, it is pointed out that automatic dishwashing may cause pitting and darkening of the aluminum interior.

There are advantages and disadvantages to most cookware. By studying use and care instructions, you can eliminate a great deal of the guesswork when picking and choosing cookware to suit a working parent's needs.

Household utensils and appliances are made of a variety of materials. The choice in any given case depends upon materials that have properties best suited for use.

There follows a listing of suggested basic cookware and kitchen tools to help the working parent cook and clean up with maximum speed and efficiency.

BASIC UTENSILS FOR EFFICIENT COOKING

Basic Top-of-Stove Cookware

3 saucepans with tight-fitting covers, 1-quart, 2-quart, 3-quart

A covered or uncovered cooking utensil with one long handle; some have a small side handle. Sizes range from 1/2-quart to 4-quart in increments of 1/2 quart.

1 large kettle or large saucepot with tight-fitting cover, size depending on size of family

A covered utensil with side handles. Sizes range from 3- to 20-quart and up.

1 Dutch oven, 4- to 4 1/2-quart	A deep cooking utensil with tight-fitting cover and 2 side handles. Sometimes equipped with a rack. Sizes available from 4-quart and up in increments of 1/2 quart.
1 double boiler, 1 1/2-quart	Two saucepans or a saucepan and an insert pan made so that one may be inserted into the other. Equipped with a cover. Sizes range from 1 1/2-quart and up in increments of 1/2 quart. Used to make custards, cream sauces, puddings, etc.
Food steamer	A unit constructed with self-adjusting perforated sides to fit into many pots and pans. Designed to take on the shape of a pot. In a saucepan, it functions as a bowl shape on legs, while in a skillet it opens up almost flat on the feet. This unit allows food to be cooked by steam without resting in water. A minimum of nutrients is lost, and two or more vegetables can be cooked at once yet maintain separate identity.
2 fry pans (skillets) with covers, 1 medium 8- or 9-inch, covered, and 1 large, 12-inch, covered	Shallow pan, covered or uncovered, with one long handle. May also have a small side handle. Sizes available from 6 to 12 inches. Measurement is top outside dimension.
1 pressure cooker, 4- or 6-quart size depending on size of family	A utensil with locked cover that utilizes pressure and steam to cook foods in one-third to one-tenth the time usually required. Sizes vary from 2- to 20-quart. However, the 4- and 6-quart sizes are generally used for home cooking. Excellent for quick stews and many other

combination main dishes, pork roasts and other meats, vegetables, soups, and desserts such as rice pudding, bread pudding, and custard. Note: Pressure cooker recipes have not been included in this book because it is advisable to follow manufacturer's instructions for cooking with this equipment.

Basic Oven Cookware
1 roasting pan with rack:
17 1/2 x 11 3/4 x 2 1/4 inches
or 15 1/2 x 10 3/4 x 2 1/4 inches
1 large casserole, 3-quart, and 1 medium casserole, 2-quart, with covers
1 bake sheet with rim:
15 1/2 x 10 1/2 x 1 inches
1 loaf pan, 9 x 5 x 3 inches
Oblong baking dishes, 2-quart and 3-quart
1 9-inch-square baking dish

Cookware for Baked Goods
1 additional loaf pan, 9 x 5 x 3 inches
2 cookie sheets; sizes range from 10 x 8 inches to 18 x 12 inches; select according to size of oven
2 9-inch-round cake pans
Muffin tins, 6 or 12 cups
2 pie pans, 9-inch

Thermometers
Refrigerator thermometer

Dial refrigerator and freezer thermometer designed to either stand or hang in the unit. Refrigerator controls indicate only the degree of cold in the refrigerator. When foods are to be kept longer than 3–4 days, it is absolutely essential that the temperature be 40° F. to insure the quality and safekeeping of the food. The refrigerator thermometer is designed especially to offer this check of your refrigerator.

Freezer thermometer

This tube-like thermometer has a bulb and is designed to hang on the partition in chest-type freezers or to rest on a flat surface in upright freezers. This thermometer registers temperature accurately to insure keeping quality of foods stored in freezer. Temperature should be 0° or below.

Oven thermometers

Two types are available: (1) A mercury tube thermometer made of metal with a mercury-filled tube for accuracy. Designed to either stand on or hang from oven rack. (2) Bimetallic oven thermometer with dial face. Designed either to stand on or hang from oven rack.

Meat thermometer

Two popular styles are: (1) Dial roast meat thermometer has a flat dial face attached to a meat probe. Units are watertight; some have preset indicators for quick check of internal meat temperature and degree of doneness. (2) Meat and yeast thermometer is flat unit with meat probe and readings for internal meat temperature and degree of doneness as well as temperature markings for yeast bread making. There are others available including styles for microwave ovens. The meat thermometer gives an accurate temperature for the inside of the meat as it cooks. It is inserted in the meat and registers the degree of doneness of all kinds of roasts, thick steaks, and chops. The meat thermometer is essential in cooking meats such as pork and poultry. Instructions for use accompany the thermometer.

Forks
2 to 3 regular forks
1 large two-pronged fork
Very small fork for removing food from narrow-necked bottles

Spoons
Wooden spoons, 2 sizes
Long-handled slotted spoon
3 to 4 regular kitchen spoons
Very small spoon for removing food from narrow-necked bottles

Knives
2 paring knives
1 slicer
1 carver
1 utility

Preparation Tools and Other Equipment
Tongs
Wire whisk or egg beater
Grater, 4-sided or flat
Juicer
Colander
Strainers, large and small
Rubber scrapers
Corkscrew
Bottle opener
Can opener
Vegetable peeler
Vegetable brush
Cutting board
Wire cooling racks

Spatula
Ladle
Pancake turner
Potato masher, if used
Dry measuring cups, 2-cup,
1-cup, 1/2-cup, 1/3-cup, 1/4-cup
Liquid measuring cups, 1-quart,
1-pint, and 1-cup
Measuring spoons

Implements for Baked Goods
Rolling pin
Biscuit cutter
Sifter
Pastry blender
Pastry brush

Bowls, Dishes, etc.
4 nested mixing bowls,
1 1/2-pint, 1 1/2-quart,
2 1/2-quart, 4-quart
1 large mixing bowl, 6- to
8-quart
Pitcher
1 or 2 platters
Ovenproof and flameproof
dishes, 2 sizes
Extra dishes and bowls,
depending upon size of family

10
How to Prevent Food Poisoning

Researchers estimate that outbreaks of salmonella infection, a common food poisoning, may mean a loss to
the United States of more than a billion dollars a year,
which includes avoidable medical expenses and loss of
productivity costs.

"Upset stomach," nausea, vomiting, abdominal
cramps, and/or diarrhea are often blamed on "a bug
that is going around" but these symptoms, individually

or together, may be caused by harmful bacteria in perishable foods. The way you handle, cook and store food can prevent illness caused by harmful bacteria in foods.

According to Food and Drug Administration Bulletin No. 74-2044, bacterial contamination of foods can be reduced through either cooking or refrigeration which retards and controls the growth of disease-producing bacteria.

Bacteria require three things to grow and multiply: warmth, moisture and a food. If any one of these is missing, bacteria do not grow. Although refrigeration does not kill most bacteria, when food is refrigerated, warmth is lacking and the bacteria growth is kept in check. Cooking foods at correct temperature and timing for the food as given in the recipe retards or kills bacteria.

Perishable food products and potentially hazardous foods require careful handling and refrigeration. Potentially hazardous foods include milk and milk products such as cheeses and ice cream, eggs, meat, poultry, fish and shellfish, and food mixtures such as cream pies, custards, potato salad, and protein food salads such as tuna, chicken, meat, etc.

Responsibility for food safety starts at the grocery store. For safe food, it is wise to develop these habits.

• Make the grocery store the last stop when shopping. Take foods directly home.

• Buy perishable foods as well as those listed above in amounts you can use in a reasonable time and in amounts you can store properly at home.

• Buy only those frozen foods which are kept below the frost line, sometimes called the load line, when displayed in open chest-type freezers. The frost line is usually marked somewhere on the inner wall of the freezer. You will also find a thermometer that is visible to the customer and is usually at the edge of the inner-wall lining. This should register 0° F. or lower. In the upright freezer chest that has a door, you will find a thermometer that should register 0° F. or below. If you are not able to find the thermometer or load line in either type of chest, ask the manager to show you where it is.

• Place refrigerated and frozen foods in your shopping basket last. Remember, the colder you keep the food, the safer it is.

Once you get home, put into practice these refrigeration rules.

• Refrigerate perishable foods immediately. Do not allow groceries to sit around in the car, or on a table or counter in the kitchen.

• Check refrigerator temperature. Make sure it is cold enough to keep foods safe. If food is to be kept for only three or four days, the temperature should be 45° F. or below. However, when there are small children in the family who open and close the refrigerator often, or when food is to be kept longer than three or four days, it is strongly recommended that the refrigerator temperature by kept at 40° F. How important is refrigerator temperature? The above-cited Food and Drug Administration bulletin emphasizes that at temperatures above 45° F. (and up to 115° F.), both infectious bacteria and toxin-producing microorganisms may grow rapidly. In fact, foods may undergo a doubling of bacterial growth every 15–20 minutes. This also shows why it is important to prepare and serve foods as quickly as possible after taking them from the refrigerator.

• Once food is prepared and served, it is important never to leave leftovers on the table or counter. They should be stored in the refrigerator immediately. An easy rule to follow is to refrigerate food before starting cleanup after dinner.

• When storing foods, it is better to store them in small, shallow (flat) containers. Foods cool faster when more of the surface is exposed to the cold.

• Leftover food should be covered when storing. This prevents food from the shelf above from falling into food stored on a lower shelf.

• The temperature of a home freezer should be kept at 0° F. or below.

• When frozen food is to be defrosted or thawed, put it in the refrigerator to thaw. Do not thaw frozen foods on table or counter space at room temperature because they can spoil easily and cause illness.

• Do not try to refreeze food unless the label expressly states that it is safe to do so.

Just as the food needs special attention and care, so

do the refrigerator and freezer. To keep them working properly, follow these suggestions.

• Wash inside of refrigerator frequently, and freezer periodically.

• Check the gaskets, or rubberlike material, around the doors. They should be flexible, keep cold air from escaping, and warm air from entering. A simple way to check is to close the door on a sheet of paper in several spots around the door. Pull paper. If it comes out easily, have the gaskets checked by a serviceman.

• The motor and refrigerating unit should be clean. Lint and dirt on these parts cut off the supply of air. When this happens, the motor and refrigerator unit are overworked.

• If your refrigerator is not self-defrosting, check the cooling area and defrost when needed. A buildup of ice on the cooling coils prevents the refrigerator from cooling properly.

• Avoid overcrowding your refrigerator. There should be air space around the food to achieve maximum cooling.

• Never cover the open wire shelves with paper or aluminum foil. This cuts down on air circulation in the refrigerator, and the food does not cool properly.

It goes without saying that hands should be clean before handling food. It is important that both the hands and the utensils should be thoroughly cleaned to prepare food, and cleaned again before handling other food. For example, after handling raw chicken and many other raw foods, the hands and utensils must be washed thoroughly before preparing another dish such as a green salad which will not be cooked before serving. The bacteria on the chicken are killed when it is thoroughly cooked. But the bacteria which remain on the hands and knife could be transferred to the salad greens which are eaten raw. That is why it is important to wash hands and implements thoroughly.

Additional safety tips:

• When cooking meats, use a meat thermometer to make sure the inside of the meat is cooked thoroughly. For example, the internal temperature for fresh pork should read at least 170° F., and for poultry, 180° F.–185°F.

• Eggs with cracked shells should never be used unless thoroughly cooked.

• Cream-filled pies and custards must be cooled properly. Fillings should be cooled immediately after they have been mixed. When cooled or baked custard is not served immediately after cooking, refrigerate it at 45° F. or below. Keep at this temperature until ready to serve. Do not remove from refrigerator and allow to stand at room temperature for too long. The same care should be taken with foods such as cream-filled pastries, meat, fish, egg and vegetable salad mixtures.

• Special care should be taken when serving and using low-acid foods such as green beans, beets or corn. These foods should be handled and stored in the same manner as other perishable foods.

• Do not use commercially canned or home-canned foods where there is swelling of container or evidence of leakage. If the food does not look right, or you think it is spoiled, do not taste it. Spoiled foods often do not change in flavor.

Foods That Are Important Sources of Nutrients

Foods are listed in descending order for each nutrient according to the percentage of the USRDA they provide. Consider the amount of food specified. It may not be the same as the amount you usually eat.

Percentages have been rounded off to the nearest percentage that would be shown on labels.

Figures from "Nutrition Labeling . . . Tools for Its Use," United States Department of Agriculture, Agricultural Information Bulletin No. 382.

VITAMIN A

Food	Percentage of USRDA	Amount of food
Meat and Meat Alternates		
Liver, beef	910	3 ounces
Liver, calf	560	3 ounces
Liver, hog	250	3 ounces
Liver, chicken	60	1 ounce
Chicken or turkey potpie, home recipe (9-inch diameter)	60	1/3 pie
Beef and vegetable stew	50	1 cup
Vegetables and Fruit		
Carrots, canned	470	1 cup
Sweetpotatoes, mashed	400	1 cup
Carrots, cooked	330	1 cup
Spinach, canned	330	1 cup
Pumpkin, canned	310	1 cup
Sweetpotatoes, pieces, canned	310	1 cup

151

Food	Percentage of USRDA	Amount of food
Collards, cooked	300	1 cup
Peas and carrots, cooked	300	1 cup
Spinach, cooked	290	1 cup
Dandelion greens, cooked	250	1 cup
Carrots, raw, grated	240	1 cup
Sweetpotato (medium), boiled in skin	240	1 potato
Turnip greens, canned, solids and liquid	220	1 cup
Cress, garden, cooked	210	1 cup
Chard, Swiss, cooked	190	1 cup
Mango, raw	190	1 fruit (2/3 pound)
Cantaloupe (5-inch diameter), raw	180	1/2 melon
Kale, cooked	180	1 cup
Mustard greens, cooked from frozen	180	1 cup
Sweetpotato (medium), baked in skin	180	1 potato
Turnip greens, cooked	180	1 cup
Vegetables, mixed, cooked	180	1 cup
Squash, winter, baked	170	1 cup
Mustard greens, cooked	160	1 cup
Apricots, dried, cooked	150	1 cup
Beet greens, cooked	150	1 cup
Cabbage, spoon, cooked	110	1 cup
Sweetpotato (3-ounce piece), candied	110	1 piece
Broccoli, chopped, cooked from frozen	100	1 cup
Apricots, canned	90	1 cup
Broccoli, cooked	90	1 medium stalk
Spinach, raw, chopped	90	1 cup
Apricots (medium), dried, uncooked	80	10 halves
Broccoli, cut, cooked	80	1 cup
Melon balls, frozen, in syrup	70	1 cup
Pepper, red	70	1 pod
Apricots, raw	60	3 fruits
Peaches, dried, cooked	60	1 cup

Food	Percentage of U.S. RDA	Amount of food
Plums, canned	60	1 cup
Carrots, strips (2½ to 3 inches long), raw	60	6–8 strips
Papaya, raw, cubed	50	1 cup
Tomatoes, cooked	50	1 cup
Watermelon wedge (4 x 8-inch) raw	50	1 wedge
Cereal and Bakery Products		
Pie, pumpkin	80	4¾-inch sector
Pie, sweetpotato	70	4¾-inch sector
Miscellaneous		
Soup:		
Vegetable, with beef broth	60	1 cup
Vegetable, vegetarian	60	1 cup
Vegetable beef	60	1 cup
Apricot nectar	50	1 cup

VITAMIN C

Food	Percentage of USRDA	Amount of food
Meat and Meat Alternates		
Peppers (6.5-ounce), stuffed	120	1 pepper
Chop suey, with beef and pork, home recipe	60	1 cup
Liver, calf	50	3 ounces
Vegetables and Fruit		
Broccoli, cooked	270	1 medium stalk
Pepper, red, raw	250	1 pod
Collards, cooked	240	1 cup
Broccoli, cut, cooked	230	1 cup
Brussels sprouts, cooked	230	1 cup
Strawberries, frozen, sweetened	230	1 cup
Pepper, green, cooked	220	1 cup
Orange juice, fresh	210	1 cup
Orange juice, from frozen or canned concentrate	200	1 cup

Food	Percentage of USRDA	Amount of food
Broccoli, chopped, cooked from frozen	180	1 cup
Kale, cooked	170	1 cup
Turnip greens, cooked	170	1 cup
Orange juice, canned	170	1 cup
Peaches, frozen	170	1 cup
Pepper, green, raw	160	1 pod
Grapefruit juice, fresh or from frozen unsweetened concentrate	160	1 cup
Cantaloupe (5-inch diameter), raw	150	½ melon
Orange sections, raw	150	1 cup
Strawberries, raw	150	1 cup
Grapefruit sections, raw, white or pink	140	1 cup
Grapefruit juice, canned, unsweetened	140	1 cup
Grapefruit juice, from frozen sweetened concentrate	140	1 cup
Grapefruit sections, canned, syrup pack	130	1 cup
Grapefruit juice, canned, sweetened	130	1 cup
Papaya, raw, cubed	130	1 cup
Grapefruit sections, canned, water pack	120	1 cup
Mango (2/3-pound), raw	120	1 fruit
Cauliflower, cooked	120	1 cup
Cauliflower, raw	110	1 cup
Mustard greens, cooked	110	1 cup
Orange (2 5/8-inch diameter), raw	110	1 orange
Tangerine juice, from frozen concentrate	110	1 cup
Tomatoes, cooked	100	1 cup
Raspberries, red, frozen	90	1 cup
Tangerine juice, canned	90	1 cup
Cabbage, cooked	80	1 cup
Cress, garden, cooked	80	1 cup
Spinach, cooked	80	1 cup

Strawberries, canned	80	1 cup
Cabbage, raw, finely shredded	70	1 cup
Cabbage, red, raw, shredded	70	1 cup
Rutabagas, cooked	70	1 cup
Tomatoes (3-inch diameter), raw	70	1 tomato
Turnip greens, canned, solids and liquid	70	1 cup
Tomato juice, canned or bottled	70	1 cup
Sauerkraut juice	70	1 cup
Grapefruit, white or pink, raw	70	1/2 medium fruit
Lemons, raw	70	1 lemon
Asparagus, pieces, cooked or canned	60	1 cup
Cabbage, common or savoy, raw, coarsely shredded	60	1 cup
Okra, sliced, cooked	60	1 cup
Peas, green, cooked	60	1 cup
Sauerkraut, canned	60	1 cup
Sweetpotatoes, canned, mashed	60	1 cup
Turnips, cooked	60	1 cup
Coleslaw	60	1 cup
Honeydew melon wedge, raw, (2 x 7-inch, 1/2-pound)	60	1 wedge
Loganberries, raw	60	1 cup
Melon balls, frozen, syrup pack	60	1 cup
Beans, lima, Fordhook, cooked from frozen	50	1 cup
Beans, lima, immature seeds, cooked	50	1 cup
Mustard greens, cooked from frozen	50	1 cup
Potato, baked in skin	50	1 medium potato
Spinach, canned	50	1 cup
Blackberries, raw	50	1 cup
Raspberries, red, raw	50	1 cup
Watermelon wedge (4 x 8-inch), raw	50	1 wedge
Pineapple juice, from frozen concentrate	50	1 cup

Food	Percentage of USRDA	Amount of food
Cereal and Bakery Products		
Spanish rice	60	1 cup
Pie, strawberry	50	4¾-inch sector
Miscellaneous		
Orange juice, from dehydrated crystals	180	1 cup
Grapefruit juice, from dehydrated crystals	150	1 cup
Cranberry juice cocktail	70	1 cup
Grape juice drink, canned	70	1 cup
Orange-apricot juice drink	70	1 cup
Pineapple-orange juice drink	70	1 cup
Pineapple-grapefruit juice drink	70	1 cup

THIAMINE

Food	Percentage of USRDA	Amount of food
Meat and Meat Alternates		
Sunflower seeds	190	1 cup
Pork, loin, chopped, lean	100	1 cup
Brazil nuts, shelled	90	1 cup
Pork, fresh or cured, ham or shoulder, chopped, lean	60	1 cup
Pork, loin, sliced, lean only	60	3 ounces
Pecans, halves	60	1 cup
Pork, loin, sliced, lean and fat	50	3 ounces
Pork, loin chop, lean and fat	50	2.7 ounces
Pork, fresh or cured, ham or shoulder, ground, lean	45	1 cup
Pork, loin chop, lean	40	2 ounces
Cashew nuts, whole kernels, roasted	40	1 cup
Filberts, whole kernels, shelled	40	1 cup

Pork, fresh or cured, ham or shoulder, sliced, lean	35	3 ounces
Pork, cured, shoulder, sliced, lean and fat	30	3 ounces
Pork, fresh, ham or shoulder, sliced, lean and fat	30	3 ounces
Kidney, beef	30	3 ounces
Peanuts	30	1 cup
Pork, cured, ham, sliced, lean and fat	25	3 ounces
Spareribs	25	3 ounces
Spaghetti (enriched) with cheese, canned	25	1 cup
Cowpeas, dry, cooked	25	1 cup
Soybeans, dry, cooked	25	1 cup
Almonds, whole, shelled	25	1 cup
Chestnuts, shelled	25	1 cup
Pumpkin kernels	25	1 cup
Walnuts, English, chopped	25	1 cup
Liver, hog	20	3 ounces
Beef potpie (9-inch), home-prepared from enriched flour	20	1/3 pie
Chicken or turkey potpie (9-inch), home-prepared from enriched flour	20	1/3 pie
Chop suey, with beef and pork, home recipe	20	1 cup
Beans, navy (pea), dry, cooked	20	1 cup
Peas, split, dry, cooked	20	1 cup
Walnuts, black, chopped	20	1 cup
Bacon, Canadian	15	1 slice
Lamb, leg or shoulder, chopped, lean	15	1 cup
Heart, beef, sliced	15	3 ounces
Liver, calf or beef	15	3 ounces
Polish sausage	15	2.4-ounce link
Pork sausage	15	1-ounce pattie or 2 links
Crab, deviled	15	1 cup
Macaroni (enriched) and cheese, home recipe	15	1 cup
Spaghetti (enriched) with cheese, home recipe	15	1 cup
Spaghetti (enriched) with meatballs, home recipe	15	1 cup

Food	Percentage of USRDA	Amount of food
Beans, canned, with pork and tomato sauce	15	1 cup
Beans, lima, Great Northern, or kidney, dry, cooked	15	1 cup
Vegetables and Fruit		
Cowpeas, cooked	35	1 cup
Peas, green, cooked	30	1 cup
Peas and carrots, cooked	20	1 cup
Beans, lima, fresh, cooked	20	1 cup
Asparagus, pieces, cooked	15	1 cup
Collards, cooked	15	1 cup
Cowpeas, canned, solids and liquid	15	1 cup
Okra, sliced, cooked	15	1 cup
Soybeans, sprouted seeds, raw or cooked	15	1 cup
Turnip greens, cooked	15	1 cup
Vegetables, mixed, cooked	15	1 cup
Potato salad, with cooked salad dressing	15	1 cup
Orange juice, fresh or from unsweetened frozen or canned concentrate	15	1 cup
Pineapple, canned, water or syrup pack	15	1 cup
Pineapple, frozen, sweetened	15	1 cup
Cereal and Bakery products		
Hoagie roll (11½-inch long), enriched	35	1 roll
Cereal, ready-to-eat (check label)	25	1 ounce
Hard roll (1.8-ounce), enriched	15	1 roll
Spoonbread	15	1 cup
Oatmeal, cooked	15	1 cup
Oat and wheat cereal, cooked	15	1 cup
Macaroni, enriched, cooked	15	1 cup

Noodles, enriched, cooked	15	1 cup
Spaghetti, enriched, cooked	15	1 cup
Rice, white, enriched, cooked	15	1 cup
Gingerbread (9-inch square), with enriched flour	15	1/9 cake
Pie (4¾-inch-sector), pecan	15	1 piece

Miscellaneous

Orange juice, from dehydrated crystals	15	1 cup
Soup, split pea	15	1 cup
Bread pudding, with enriched bread	15	1 cup

RIBOFLAVIN

Food	Percentage of USRDA	Amount of food
Milk and Milk Products		
Cheese, cottage	35	1 cup
Milk, partially skimmed	30	1 cup
Malted beverage	30	1 cup
Custard, baked	30	1 cup
Milk, whole or skim	25	1 cup
Milk, nonfat dry, reconstituted	25	1 cup
Buttermilk	25	1 cup
Chocolate drink	25	1 cup
Cocoa	25	1 cup
Ice milk, soft-serve	25	1 cup
Pudding, from mixes, with milk	25	1 cup
Pudding, vanilla, home recipe	25	1 cup
Rennin desserts	25	1 cup
Yogurt	25	1 cup
Ice cream, soft-serve	20	1 cup
Pudding, chocolate, home recipe	20	1 cup
Tapioca cream	20	1 cup

Food	Percentage of USRDA	Amount of food
Meat and Meat Alternates		
Kidney, beef	240	3 ounces
Liver, hog	220	3 ounces
Liver, beef or calf	210	3 ounces
Almonds, whole	80	1 cup
Fish loaf	60	1 slice
(4⅛ x 2½ x 1-inch)		
Heart, beef, sliced	60	3 ounces
Almonds, sliced	50	1 cup
Liver, chicken	40	1 ounce
Beef, dried, chipped, creamed	30	1 cup
Welsh rarebit	30	1 cup
Lamb, leg or shoulder, chopped, lean	25	1 cup
Pork, fresh, ham or loin, chopped, lean	25	1 cup
Veal, stewed or roasted, chopped	25	1 cup
Braunschweiger	25	1 ounce
Chicken a la king, home recipe	25	1 cup
Macaroni (enriched) and cheese, home recipe	25	1 cup
Beef, chuck or rump, chopped, lean	20	1 cup
Lamb, leg or shoulder, chopped, lean and fat	20	1 cup
Pork, cured, ham or shoulder, chopped, lean	20	1 cup
Pork, fresh, shoulder, chopped	20	1 cup
Pork, fresh, ham or shoulder, ground, lean	20	1 cup
Veal, loin, chopped	20	1 cup
Veal, rib, ground	20	1 cup
Turkey, dark meat, chopped	20	1 cup
Chicken or turkey potpie (9-inch), home-prepared from enriched flour	20	1/3 pie
Chop suey with beef and pork, home recipe	20	1 cup

Pepper (6.5-ounce), stuffed	20	1 pepper
Spaghetti (enriched) with meatballs, home recipe	20	1 cup

Vegetables and Fruit

Broccoli, cooked	20	1 medium stalk
Broccoli, cut, cooked	20	1 cup
Corn pudding	20	1 cup
Collards, cooked	20	1 cup
Turnip greens, cooked	20	1 cup
Avocado, Florida, raw	20	½ fruit
Avocado, Florida or California, raw, cubed	20	1 cup

Cereal and Bakery Products

Cereals, ready-to-eat (check label)	25	1 ounce
Spoonbread	25	1 cup
Hoagie roll (11½-inch-long), enriched	20	1 roll

Miscellaneous

Bread pudding, with enriched bread	35	1 cup
Oyster stew, home recipe	25	1 cup
Rice pudding	20	1 cup
Soup, cream of mushroom, with milk	20	1 cup

NIACIN

Food	Percentage of USRDA	Amount of food
Meat and Meat Alternates		
Peanuts	120	1 cup
Liver, hog	100	3 ounces
Chicken, light meat, chopped	80	1 cup
Turkey, light meat, chopped	80	1 cup
Liver, calf or beef	70	3 ounces
Chicken breast, (3.3-ounce piece)	60	1 piece
Chicken, stewed, dark meat, chopped	60	1 cup
Veal rib, chopped	60	1 cup
Tuna, canned in water	60	3 ounces

Food	Percentage of USRDA	Amount of food
Chicken, roasted, light meat, sliced	50	3 ounces
Turkey, canned	50	1 cup
Rabbit, domesticated	50	3 ounces
Tuna, canned in oil, drained	50	3 ounces
Tuna salad	50	1 cup
Lamb, leg, chopped, lean	45	1 cup
Kidney, beef	45	3 ounces
Pork, loin, chopped, lean	45	1 cup
Veal, stewed, chopped	45	1 cup
Veal, rib, ground	45	1 cup
Chicken, canned	45	1 cup
Chicken, stewed, light meat, sliced	45	3 ounces
Turkey, light meat, sliced	45	3 ounces
Swordfish, broiled	45	3 ounces
Chicken, broiled	40	3 ounces
Goose	40	3 ounces
Lamb, shoulder, chopped, lean	40	1 cup
Pork, fresh, ham, chopped, lean	40	1 cup
Veal, loin, chopped	40	1 cup
Turkey potpie (9-inch), home-prepared from enriched flour	40	1/3 pie
Salmon steak, broiled or baked	40	3 ounces
Sunflower seeds	40	1 cup
Beef, rump, chopped, lean	35	1 cup
Pork, fresh or cured, shoulder, chopped, lean	35	1 cup
Veal, rib, sliced	35	3 ounces
Heart, beef, sliced	35	3 ounces
Chicken, stewed, dark meat, sliced	35	3 ounces
Chicken, roasted, dark meat, chopped	35	1 cup
Halibut, broiled	35	3 ounces
Mackerel, broiled	35	3 ounces
Rockfish, oven-steamed	35	3 ounces

Shad, baked	35	3 ounces
Beef, chuck, chopped	30	1 cup
Beef, rump, ground, lean	30	1 cup
Pork, cured, ham, chopped, lean	30	1 cup
Pork, cured, shoulder, ground, lean	30	1 cup
Pork, loin, sliced, lean	30	3 ounces
Chicken fricassee, home recipe	30	1 cup
Turkey, dark meat, chopped	30	1 cup
Salmon, pink, canned	30	3 ounces
Beef potpie (9-inch), home-prepared from enriched flour	30	1/3 pie
Beef, chuck, ground, lean	25	1 cup
Beef, steak (club, porterhouse, T-bone, or sirloin), lean	25	3 ounces
Beef, steak (round)	25	3 ounces
Ground beef	25	3 ounces
Lamb, leg, sliced	25	3 ounces
Lamb, loin chop, lean and fat	25	3.5 ounces
Lamb, shoulder, sliced, lean	25	3 ounces
Pork, cured, ham, ground, lean	25	3 ounces
Pork, fresh, ham, sliced, lean	25	3 ounces
Pork, loin chop, lean and fat	25	2.7 ounces
Pork, loin, sliced, lean and fat	25	3 ounces
Veal, stewed, sliced	25	3 ounces
Veal, loin or cutlet	25	3 ounces
Chicken, roasted, dark meat, sliced	25	3 ounces
Chicken a la king, home recipe	25	1 cup
Chicken potpie (9-inch), home-prepared from enriched flour	25	1/3 pie
Salmon, red, canned	25	3 ounces
Salmon rice loaf (6-ounce piece)	25	1 piece
Sardines, canned, drained	25	3 ounces

Food	Percentage of USRDA	Amount of food
Beef and vegetable stew, home recipe	25	1 cup
Chop suey, with beef and pork, home recipe	25	1 cup
Corned beef hash, canned	25	1 cup
Peppers (6.5-ounce), stuffed	25	1 pepper
Spaghetti (enriched) with cheese, canned	25	1 cup
Beef, chuck, sliced	20	3 ounces
Beef, rump, sliced	20	3 ounces
Beef, rib, sliced, lean and fat	20	3 ounces
Beef, flank steak	20	3 ounces
Beef, plate, lean	20	3 ounces
Beef, steak (club, porterhouse, T-bone, or sirloin), lean and fat	20	3 ounces
Lamb, rib chop, lean and fat	20	3.2 ounces
Lamb, loin chop, lean	20	2.3 ounces
Lamb, shoulder, sliced, lean and fat	20	3 ounces
Pork, cured, ham, sliced, lean	20	3 ounces
Pork, fresh, ham, sliced, lean and fat	20	3 ounces
Pork, fresh or cured, shoulder, sliced	20	3 ounces
Pork, loin chop, lean	20	2 ounces
Chicken thigh, (2.3-ounce piece)	20	1 piece
Turkey, dark meat, sliced	20	3 ounces
Chicken and noodles, home recipe	20	1 cup
Chow mein, home recipe	20	1 cup
Spaghetti (enriched) with meatballs, home recipe	20	1 cup
Lobster Newburg	20	1 cup
Crab, deviled	20	1 cup

Vegetables and Fruits

Food	Percentage of USRDA	Amount of food
Dates, pitted, chopped	20	1 cup

Peaches, dried, cooked, unsweetened	20	1 cup
Peas, green, cooked	20	1 cup
Cereal and Bakery Products		
Hoagie roll (11 ½-inch-long), enriched	25	1 roll
Cereals, ready-to-eat (check label)	20	1 ounce

CALCIUM

Food	Percentage of USRDA	Amount of food
Milk and Milk Products		
Cheese, Parmesan, grated	40	1 ounce
Milk, partially skimmed	35	1 cup
Pudding, uncooked, from mix	35	1 cup
Milk, whole or skim	30	1 cup
Milk, nonfat dry, reconstituted	30	1 cup
Buttermilk	30	1 cup
Chocolate drink, made from whole milk	30	1 cup
Cocoa	30	1 cup
Malted beverage	30	1 cup
Custard, baked	30	1 cup
Pudding, vanilla, home recipe	30	1 cup
Rennin desserts	30	1 cup
Yogurt, made from partially skimmed milk	30	1 cup
Chocolate drink, made from skim milk	25	1 cup
Cheese, cottage, creamed	25	1 cup
Cheese, Swiss	25	1 ounce
Yogurt, made from whole milk	25	1 cup
Ice cream or ice milk, soft-serve	25	1 cup
Pudding, cooked, from mix, with milk	25	1 cup
Pudding, chocolate, home recipe	25	1 cup

Food	Percentage of USRDA	Amount of food
Cheese, American, process	20	1 ounce
Cheese, Cheddar, natural	20	1 ounce
Cheese, cottage, uncreamed	20	1 cup
Ice cream or ice milk, hardened	20	1 cup
Meat and Meat Alternates		
Welsh rarebit	60	1 cup
Sardines, canned, drained	35	3 ounces
Macaroni (enriched) and cheese, home recipe	35	1 cup
Potatoes au gratin	30	1 cup
Beef, dried, chipped, creamed	25	1 cup
Cheese soufflé	20	1 cup
Lobster Newburg	20	1 cup
Macaroni (enriched) and cheese, canned	20	1 cup
Vegetables and Fruit		
Collards, cooked	35	1 cup
Cabbage, spoon, cooked	25	1 cup
Spinach, canned	25	1 cup
Turnip greens	25	1 cup
Kale, cooked	20	1 cup
Mustard greens, cooked	20	1 cup
Rhubarb, cooked	20	1 cup
Cereal and Bakery Products		
Spoonbread	25	1 cup
Farina, enriched, instant	20	1 cup
Miscellaneous		
Bread pudding	30	1 cup
Oyster stew, home recipe	30	1 cup
Rice pudding	25	1 cup
Soup, with milk:		
Green pea	20	1 cup
Cream of celery	20	1 cup
Cream of mushroom	20	1 cup
Cream of asparagus	20	1 cup

IRON

Food	Percentage of USRDA	Amount of food
Meat and Meat Alternates		
Liver, hog	140	3 ounces
Pumpkin kernels	90	1 cup
Liver, calf	70	3 ounces
Kidney, beef	60	3 ounces
Sunflower seeds	60	1 cup
Liver, beef	40	3 ounces
Walnuts, black, chopped	40	1 cup
Clams, canned, drained, chopped	35	1 cup
Beans, lima, dry, cooked	35	1 cup
Beans, with pork and sweet sauce, canned	35	1 cup
Almonds, whole, shelled	35	1 cup
Beef, chuck or rump, chopped, lean	30	1 cup
Pork, cured, shoulder, chopped, lean	30	1 cup
Pork, fresh, ham or loin, chopped, lean	30	1 cup
Heart, beef, sliced	30	3 ounces
Clams, raw	30	4 or 5 clams
Beef potpie (9-inch), home-prepared from enriched flour	30	1/3 pie
Beans, navy (pea), dry, cooked	30	1 cup
Beans, white, dry, canned, solids and liquids	30	1 cup
Cashew nuts, whole kernels, roasted	30	1 cup
Beef, chuck or rump, ground, lean	25	1 cup
Pork, cured, ham, chopped, lean	25	1 cup
Pork, fresh, shoulder, chopped	25	1 cup
Pork, fresh, ham, ground, lean	25	1 cup

Food	Percentage of USRDA	Amount of food
Veal, chopped	25	1 cup
Chicken or turkey potpie, (9-inch), home-prepared from enriched flour	25	1/3 pie
Chile con carne with beans, canned	25	1 cup
Chop suey, with beef and pork, home recipe	25	1 cup
Corned beef hash, canned	25	1 cup
Beans, Great Northern or red kidney, dry, cooked	25	1 cup
Beans, red kidney, dry, canned, solids and liquid	25	1 cup
Lentils, dry, cooked	25	1 cup
Soybeans, dry, cooked	25	1 cup
Beans, with frankfurters, canned	25	1 cup
Beans, with pork and tomato sauce, canned	25	1 cup
Beef, chuck, sliced, lean	20	3 ounces
Beef, flank steak	20	3 ounces
Beef, plate, lean	20	3 ounces
Beef, steak, sirloin, lean	20	3 ounces
Pork, cured, ham or shoulder, ground, lean	20	1 cup
Pork, fresh, shoulder, ground, lean	20	1 cup
Pork, fresh, ham, sliced, lean	20	3 ounces
Pork, loin, sliced, lean	20	3 ounces
Turkey, dark meat, chopped	20	1 cup
Veal, rib, ground	20	1 cup
Peppers (6.5-ounce), stuffed	20	1 pepper
Spaghetti (enriched) in tomato sauce, with meatballs; canned or home-prepared	20	1 cup

Cowpeas, dry, cooked	20	1 cup
Peas, split, dry, cooked	20	1 cup
Beef, chuck, lean and fat, sliced	15	3 ounces
Beef, corned	15	3 ounces
Beef, plate, lean and fat	15	3 ounces
Beef, rump, sliced	15	3 ounces
Beef, rib, sliced, lean	15	3 ounces
Beef, steak (round)	15	3 ounces
Beef, steak (club, porterhouse, or T-bone), lean	15	3 ounces
Beef, steak (sirloin), lean and fat	15	3 ounces
Ground beef	15	3 ounces
Lamb, shoulder, chopped, lean	15	1 cup
Lamb, leg, chopped	15	1 cup
Pork, cured, shoulder, sliced	15	3 ounces
Pork, cured, ham, sliced, lean	15	3 ounces
Pork, fresh, loin or ham, sliced, lean and fat	15	3 ounces
Pork, loin chop, lean and fat	15	2.7 ounces
Pork, fresh, shoulder, sliced	15	3 ounces
Veal, sliced	15	3 ounces
Veal, cutlet or loin	15	3 ounces
Beef and vegetable stew, home recipe	15	1 cup
Chicken, dark meat, chopped	15	1 cup
Chicken, canned	15	1 cup
Spaghetti (enriched) with tomato sauce and cheese, canned	15	1 cup
Turkey, canned	15	1 cup
Chow mein, chicken, home recipe	15	1 cup
Chicken a la king, home recipe	15	1 cup
Crab, deviled	15	1 cup
Sardines, canned	15	3 ounces

Food	Percentage of USRDA	Amount of food
Shrimp, canned	15	3 ounces
Tuna salad	15	1 cup
Vegetables and Fruit		
Peaches, dried, uncooked	60	1 cup
Prune juice, canned	60	1 cup
Dates, pitted, chopped	30	1 cup
Raisins, seedless	30	1 cup
Spinach, canned	30	1 cup
Asparagus, pieces, canned	25	1 cup
Beans, lima, canned	25	1 cup
Beans, lima, fresh or frozen, baby, cooked	25	1 cup
Apricots, dried, cooked	25	1 cup
Peaches, dried, cooked	25	1 cup
Cowpeas, cooked	20	1 cup
Cowpeas, canned, solids and liquid	20	1 cup
Peas, green, canned	20	1 cup
Spinach, cooked	20	1 cup
Turnip greens, canned, solids and liquid	20	1 cup
Prunes, dried, cooked	20	1 cup
Beans, lima, Fordhook, cooked	15	1 cup
Beet greens, cooked	15	1 cup
Chard, Swiss, cooked	15	1 cup
Mustard greens, fresh or frozen, cooked	15	1 cup
Peas, green, cooked	15	1 cup
Sauerkraut juice	15	1 cup
Vegetables, mixed, cooked	15	1 cup
Boysenberries, canned	15	1 cup
Plums, canned, water or syrup pack	15	1 cup
Prunes, dried, uncooked	15	10 prunes
Cereal and Bakery Products		
Farina, instant, enriched, cooked	90	1 cup

Farina, regular and quick-cooking, enriched, cooked	70	1 cup
Hoagie roll (11 1/2-inch-long), enriched	40	1 roll
Cereals, ready-to-eat (check label)	20	1 ounce
Cottage pudding (8-inch-square), with enriched flour and chocolate sauce	20	1/6 cake
Gingerbread (9-inch-square), with enriched flour	20	1/9 cake
Pie (4¾-inch sector), pecan	20	1 piece
Coffeecake (2.5-ounce-piece), with enriched flour	15	1 piece
Cottage pudding (8-inch-square), with enriched flour and strawberry sauce	15	1/6 cake
Hard roll (1.8-ounce), enriched	15	1 roll
Spoonbread	15	1 cup

Miscellaneous

Bread pudding, with raisins and enriched bread	20	1 cup
Oyster stew, home recipe	20	1 cup
Molasses, blackstrap	20	1 tablespoon
Apple brown betty, with enriched bread	15	1 cup
Syrup, sorghum	15	1 tablespoon

KEY NUTRIENTS

Nutrients/What They Do	*Food Sources*
PROTEINS Build and repair all body tissues. Help form antibodies to fight infections. Help build blood. Supply energy (calories). Form an important part of hormones and enzymes which affect metabolism.	Animal (complete) proteins: Milks, cheese, eggs, fish, poultry, meats. Plant (incomplete) proteins: Bread, cereals, other grain products, legumes (beans, peas, lentils, garbanzos, and peanuts), nuts such as walnuts, pecans, etc.
CARBOHYDRATES Supply energy. Help body to use other nutrients. Some provide cellulose (also known as fiber, bulk or roughage).	Starches: Grains, such as wheat, corn, oats and rice, products made from grains, such as flour, pasta products, breads, and breakfast cereals. Potatoes, sweetpotatoes, dry beans and peas as well as fruits and vegetables. Sugars: Cane and beet sugars, jelly, jams, honey and other sweeteners and sweets.
FATS Help body use other nutrients. Form protective cushioning around vital organs. Provide energy. Some supply essential fatty acids.	Butter, margarine, shortening, cooking and salad oils, lard, cream, most cheeses, salad dressings, nuts, mayonnaise. Meats, especially bacon. Whole milk, eggs, peanut butter, chocolate, avocados, olives.

Nutrients/What They Do	Food Sources

CALCIUM

Helps build bones and teeth. Helps blood to clot. Helps nerves and muscles to react normally. Helps proper functioning of heart.

Milk, natural cheese, other cheddar-type cheese, ice cream.

Dark green vegetables such as kale, collards, turnip and mustard greens.

Canned salmon, if bones are eaten, canned sardines.

IRON

Combines with protein to make hemoglobin, the red part of blood that carries oxygen to the cells. Helps cells use oxygen.

Liver, lean meats, heart, kidney, shellfish.

Dry beans, dry peas.

Dark green leafy vegetables.

Dried fruit such as prunes.

Egg and egg yolk.

Whole grain and enriched breads and cereals.

IODINE

Prevents goiter, the swelling of the thyroid gland.

Iodized salt.

Shellfish.

All saltwater fish.

VITAMIN A

Promotes normal growth and tissue repair. Helps keep the skin and inner linings of the body healthy and resistant to infection. Maintains healthy eyes and normal vision in dim light (protects against night blindness).

Animal sources (Vitamin A): Liver, eggs, butter, whole milk, cheese made with whole milk, fish liver oils.

Vegetable sources (carotene which body changes to Vitamin A): Dark yellow vegetables and fruits such as carrots, winter squash, sweet potatoes, apricots, papayas, cantaloupes, and mangos. Dark green leafy vegetables, such as spinach, chard, beet greens, kale, collards. Broccoli, tomatoes.

Margarine.

Nutrients/What They Do	*Food Sources*

VITAMIN D

Helps build strong bones and teeth. Helps body to absorb and use calcium and phosphorus. Prevents and cures rickets.

Fish liver oils.

Vitamin D–fortified milk.

VITAMIN C

Prevents scurvy. Helps form and maintain cementing material that holds body cells together and strengthens the walls of blood vessels. Essential to the proper absorption of iron and activity of folacin. Assists in normal tooth and bone formation and aids in healing wounds. Contributes to maintaining healthy gums and teeth.

Citrus fruits, such as oranges, grapefruit, tangerines, lemons, and their juices.

Fresh strawberries, tomatoes and juice.

Broccoli, brussels sprouts, cabbage, green peppers, some dark green leafy vegetables, such as collards, kale, spinach, and mustard greens.

Potatoes and sweetpotatoes cooked in skin.

Guavas and rose hips.

VITAMIN B_1 (THIAMINE)

Helps promote normal appetite and digestion. Helps body release energy from food. Essential to normal growth. Needed for proper function of heart, nerves and muscles.

Whole grains, germ of grain, enriched grain products, such as bread and breakfast cereals.

Meat (especially pork, liver, heart and kidney).

Soybeans, peanuts, dry peas and beans, some other nuts.

Sunflower seeds.

Green leafy vegetables, such as collards, turnip greens.

Nutrients/What They Do	*Food Sources*
VITAMIN B$_2$ (RIBOFLAVIN) Aids metabolism of carbohydrate and protein. Helps keep skin and eyes healthy.	Liver and meat. Milk, cheese. Dark green leafy vegetables, such as turnip greens and collards as well as broccoli. Whole-grain and enriched cereals and flour.
NIACIN Helps to maintain normal function of nervous and digestive systems. Prevents pellagra. Helps cells use other nutrients.	Liver, meat, fish. Whole-grain and enriched cereals and flour. Dried peas and beans, and some nuts. Peanut butter.
VITAMIN B$_6$ Works with enzymes to help the body use food, as in the conversion of the amino acid tryptophan to the vitamin niacin. Essential in metabolism of fat, proteins, carbohydrates.	Whole grain cereals, wheat germ, bran, oatmeal. Bananas, prunes and raisins. Lean meat, liver, kidney. Soybeans, split peas, peanuts. Most dark green leafy vegetables. Most fish and shellfish.
VITAMIN B$_{12}$ Beneficial in pernicious anemia. Essential for normal growth and functioning of all body cells. Involved in red blood cell formation.	Present in foods of animal origin. Kidney, liver, meat. Most fish, shellfish. Milk, most cheese. Egg and egg yolk.
FOLACIN Essential for normal, healthy blood. Essential for growth. Related to function of Vitamin B$_{12}$.	Green leafy vegetables. Whole grain cereals, wheat germ. Dry beans and nuts. Liver.

Index